energize your company with empathy

Mike Larkin & Diane Shea-Larkin

Published in 2000 by Stoddart Publishing Co. Limited
34 Lesmill Road, Toronto, Canada M3B 2T6
180 Varick Street, 9th Floor, New York, New York 10014

Distributed in Canada by:
General Distribution Services Ltd.
325 Humber College Blvd., Toronto, Ontario M9W 7C3
Tel. (416) 213-1919   Fax (416) 213-1917
Email cservice@genpub.com

Distributed in the United States by:
General Distribution Services Inc.
PMB 128, 4500 Witmer Industrial Estates,
Niagara Falls, New York 14305-1386
Toll-free Tel.1-800-805-1083   Toll-free Fax 1-800-481-6207
Email gdsinc@genpub.com

04 03 02 01 00 1 2 3 4 5

Canadian Cataloguing in Publication Data
Larkin, Mike, 1950–
CARE: energize your company with empathy

ISBN 0-7737-6143-8

1. Industrial management.   I. Shea-Larkin, Diane.   II. Title
HD31.L3156 2000   658.4   C00-931326-5

U.S. Cataloging-in-Publication Data
(Library of Congress Standards)
Larkin, Mike.
CARE : energize your company with empathy / Mike Larkin and Diane Shea-Larkin. —1st ed.
[144]p. : cm.
Summary: CARE utilizes four principles: Clear direction and support, Adequate and appropriate training, Recognition and reward, and Empathy.
ISBN 0-7737-6143-8 (pbk.)
1. Personnel management.   2. Quality of work life.
3. Organizational effectiveness.   I. Shea-Larkin, Diane.   II. Title.
658.3 21 2000   CIP

Cover Design: Mark Weir
Text Design: Tannice Goddard

THE CANADA COUNCIL | LE CONSEIL DES ARTS
FOR THE ARTS | DU CANADA
SINCE 1957 | DEPUIS 1957

We acknowledge for their financial support of our
publishing program the Canada Council, the Ontario Arts
Council, and the Government of Canada through the
Book Publishing Industry Development Program (BPIDP).

Printed and bound in Canada

For our parents,
Joe and Ivy Shea, and Joe and Adrienne Larkin.
Thanks for your love and guidance,
and for teaching us how to CARE.

Contents

Preface

CARE is the product of our respective childhoods and our work experience. Both of us were fortunate to have had parents who truly cared about us — and they demonstrated their care every day. We were given clear expectations, we were shown how to do things, we were rewarded for good behavior, and we were reprimanded when we did not meet their expectations. Most of all, our parents *listened* to us — whether we were telling them what happened at school that day, or explaining what we wanted to do in life. They always seemed to have the knack of remembering what it was like when they were "that age." They could therefore empathize and, when it was called for, give great advice.

As we entered the workforce, we expected that bosses and employees would care about each other for their mutual benefit. But, of course, our naivete was quickly put to rest as we found that not everyone feels and acts this way! Among the managers were some "CARE managers," as we began to refer to them. They stood out from the pack. Everyone wanted to work for them. And their teams always seemed to achieve the best results. But many of the managers were non-caring. It wasn't that they were nasty, though such people are always with us, at the office and everywhere else. It was that they just didn't get it. They were decent human beings who wanted to do a good job, wanted to motivate their staff to do great things, and maybe even wanted to be well liked along the way. But it just didn't come naturally to them. They needed to be taught the basic principles of achieving through others — not by intimidation, but with empathy.

This insight into management problems evolved over several years. The topic was tossed about over our dinner table for several more. Then one of us was called on to help resolve a management-employee issue. The first CARE workshop was created to address the immediate problem — and it was successful. Larger versions of the seminar followed. Each became a little more sophisticated and detailed, with a growing emphasis on follow-through. These efforts were nonetheless greeted with heartfelt praise by participants, all of whom acknowledged a sense of personal resonance. This validation of our CARE principles ultimately led to the writing of this book.

We would like to sincerely thank our first CARE managers — our parents — as well as the many truly caring individuals with whom we have had the privilege to work over the past 25 years. We hope that the essence of CARE, embodied in this book, will not only change the way you interact with others in the workplace, but will enhance every aspect of your life. Take care.

Mike and Diane

1

It's All about CARE

ZIMCO, WESTERN DIVISION, LOS ANGELES

Will Riley glanced at his watch for the fifth time in the last three minutes. *Where the hell was she?* In less than two hours he was scheduled to meet the new company president, Matt McMaster, to deliver a status report on the Wilson project, and his *trusty* assistant, Molly, was nowhere to be found. Fuming, Will reached for his phone and tried Molly's home number for the third time that morning.

On the third ring, a clearly out-of-breath Molly answered, "Hello?"

"Hello? That's it? HELLO? You're almost an hour late for work! I'm on with McMaster at 11:00. YOU KNOW THAT! And you're sitting around the house taking phone calls?"

"Mr. Riley, I can explain —"

Riley interrupted, "I don't want explanations, Molly, I want action!"

"But —"

"The only 'BUT' I want is YOURS — IN HERE, NOW!"

Before Molly could reply, Will slammed the phone back into its cradle. He shook his head and demanded of his empty office, "How can I run my division with support like this?"

In her apartment bedroom, Molly Shannon gently hung up her phone. She looked at her four-year-old son resting comfortably at last in her bed, and started to cry. Molly had been up most of the night with Liam, nursing him through a very bad cold and a painful ear infection. This was the second night in a row that she had been up with him, and she was exhausted. A single mother, Molly had no one else to turn to for help in caring for her little boy. She had planned to get to work on time, but then her nanny had called in sick that morning. Molly had been forced to scramble to find somebody to babysit, and the sitter she'd hired was due to arrive any minute. She knew she should have phoned Riley and told him she would be late, but she just couldn't bring herself to make the call. She knew he wouldn't listen and would scream at her, exactly as he had done this morning. She hated him, but she needed the job and didn't have time to look for another one. Her tears were interrupted by the sound of the doorbell. Liam's sitter had finally arrived.

Twenty minutes later, Molly Shannon climbed aboard the commuter train that would take her most of the 45

miles she traveled each day to her job. On most days she read material for the university correspondence course she was taking. Today, however, she planned to work on the report that her boss needed for his meeting with the new company president. Had Riley taken the time to listen to her during his angry tirade that morning, she could have told him that she had worked on the report throughout the night, during the periods when Liam had drifted off to sleep.

Molly opened her laptop. She was pretty sure she could finish the report by the time she arrived at her destination.

❖

ZIMCO, CENTRAL DIVISION, CHICAGO

Burt Thatcher was staring at the blank screen on his computer. The deadline was fast approaching for the channel strategy report he had been asked to prepare by his boss, Stan Cox, and Burt was still unclear about exactly what he was supposed to be doing. He had tried to get some clarification from Stan earlier in the week, but the ten minutes they had spent together had only served to confuse him further.

It wasn't that Stan was a bad boss. He had a lot of strengths: he was honest and loyal to his staff, he had an excellent, creative mind and, in general, he was a very nice guy. He was just all over the map, seeming to change his mind about what he required of his people almost daily.

Burt sighed and started tapping away on his keyboard. All he could do was give it his best shot.

❖

Stan Cox was on the phone with his new boss, Matt McMaster, when Burt appeared in his doorway for their scheduled appointment. Stan waved Burt into his office and held up two fingers, indicating he'd be free in a couple of minutes.

"Absolutely right, Matt, I couldn't agree with you more," Stan said, motioning Burt to take a seat. "Uhhuh. . . Okay, I'll see you at three tomorrow. I look forward to it."

Stan hung up and joined Burt at the worktable in the corner of his office. "How you doin', buddy?"

"No complaints. I take it that was the new boss."

"Yeah, he seems like a pretty nice guy. I'm meeting him for the first time tomorrow."

"Great. I've completed the channel strategy report you wanted."

Stan looked puzzled.

"Remember? We talked about it briefly a few days ago. You asked me to come up with some ideas about our channel strategy as it relates to our potential acquisition of Bryce Industries."

"Oh, right, right! Actually, we killed that deal a couple of days ago."

"We're not acquiring Bryce?"

"No, it looked pretty positive for a bit, but we uncovered a few things in the due diligence process that made the deal unpalatable."

"Okay, well. . ." Burt pointed to the 20-page report

he had placed in front of his boss, "I guess we won't be needing this."

"Oh . . . sorry, Burt, I thought you would have heard about the Bryce deal. Everybody's been talking about it."

"No, no . . . but that's okay. I learned quite a bit writing this, and I'm sure it will come in handy some day."

"Good."

There was a soft rap on the doorframe of Stan's office. The two men looked up to see Jennifer, Stan's assistant.

"Sorry to interrupt, Stan," Jennifer said. "I have Andy Allen on the phone. He says it's important."

"Oh, sure, put him through."

Moments later the hands-free phone on the worktable rang. Stan answered, "Andy, I'm here with Burt. What's up?"

"Sorry to interrupt, guys. Stan, I'm trying to finalize the discount rates I want to include in the Marlin Technologies bid. You were going to talk to Ursula at Nordland to see if you could squeeze her for a better price on their components. They're only offering us 15 points and we need to get them to give us another 10."

"Oh, right. Actually I haven't reached her yet. I'll try to reach her when I'm finished here with Burt. When's the bid due?"

"Tomorrow morning at 9:00. We have to get it out by priority courier tonight, no later than 7:00."

"Okay, I'll get back to you."

Burt looked across the room at his boss. The scene was all too familiar. He knew that Andy wouldn't hear another word from Stan, and the bid would go in with the 15-percent discount they currently got from Nordland. Stan just couldn't be counted on to provide support when it was really needed.

ZIMCO, NORTHERN DIVISION, TORONTO

Donna Maples scanned the presentation that her assistant, Betty, had prepared for her. It was a disaster! Donna reached under the desk and pressed her favorite office device. Moments later, in response to Donna's buzzer, Betty knocked politely and then slowly entered her boss's office.

"Betty," Donna dropped the offending presentation onto her desk from high enough to make a rather dramatic point, "this is an absolute mess."

"Oh . . . I'm sorry, Donna, I . . ."

Donna wasn't listening. "The format is all wrong. And the chart I asked you to prepare to illustrate the dramatic improvement in our inventory stockpiles is totally out of scale. McMaster wouldn't even raise an eyebrow in response to this picture." Donna flipped through the presentation while Betty stood red-faced in front of Donna's imposing oak desk.

"And look at this," Donna continued. "It's totally bland. I want some illustrations here — something dramatic."

Donna looked at her watch. "Thankfully, I'm not meeting with McMaster until tomorrow, so you'll have time to fix this." She handed the presentation to her assistant.

"Do something about the font, too — and a little color wouldn't hurt. Have this back to me by 3:00 this afternoon."

Betty took the presentation and without a word retreated from Donna's office. She felt about two inches high and she hated her boss for making her feel that way. She had tried to explain to Donna that she had not been trained in the intricacies of the computer software she had to use. On a couple of occasions she had asked if she could go on a training course, but Donna's answer was always the same: "You're here to work, not to take courses at company expense. If you want to learn what you need to know, do it on your time and on your own dollar." Betty had young children, and her aging parents were beginning to need a lot of care. She knew she needed training, but she also knew she just didn't have the time, or the money, to invest in it. She sighed and shook her head. *A degree in journalism and here I am, reduced to a glorified clerk for a woman I can't stand.*

ZIMCO, SOUTHERN DIVISION, DALLAS

Zack Daniels had been delighted when the head of his division, Paul Washington, had asked him to prepare the division overview Paul needed to review with the new company president, Matt McMaster. Zack had put a lot of effort into pulling together the overview and he was confident that the results showed.

"Zack, this is absolutely outstanding," Paul said as he handed the report back to his top regional manager. "You've really captured the essence of what we've accomplished here in Southern Division."

"Thanks, Paul."

"Just one thing . . . Since this is my review, I'd like to change the name on the bottom here to mine."

Zack's eyes focused on the name beside "Prepared by" on the report's covering page. *Zack Daniels.* "Sure, Paul," he replied in a dejected tone that was lost on his boss. "I'll do that now and get it back to you in a few minutes."

Zack left Washington's office frustrated but not surprised. Paul Washington had a reputation for passing off other people's work as his own. This had happened to Zack on more than one occasion and he was tired of it. He knew he was ready for a division manager's job, but he also knew he was never going to get the kind of recognition he needed for a promotion as long as he was working for Paul.

ZIMCO, EASTERN DIVISION, NEW YORK
Chelsea Vail slipped out of her office and walked over to Bob Tyler's desk. There was no sign of her assistant manager. It wasn't like Bob to be late, particularly when he knew that Chelsea was meeting with Matt McMaster for

the first time that morning, and that McMaster was expecting an update on an important project of Bob's. Chelsea knew enough about the Warren project to wing it, but that wasn't exactly the impression she wanted to make on the new boss. She really needed that update presentation. She reached for the phone on Bob's desk and dialed his cellular number. Bob answered on the second ring.

"Bob, it's Chelsea."

"Chelsea . . . Oh, sorry, I should have called. What time is it? Oh . . . Look, I'm on my way. I can be —"

Chelsea interrupted the young man. "Bob, slow down for a minute." The warmth in her tone was evident. "Is everything okay?"

"Sure . . ." Bob paused before continuing. "No. No, I guess things aren't exactly okay." He sounded defeated.

"What's wrong?"

Bob took a deep breath before replying, "It's my daughter. The poor kid is really sick. We spent most of the night at children's Hospital. I just got home about five minutes ago."

"Is Alison going to be all right?"

"The doctor says she'll be fine. Apparently she picked up this new Asian flu strain that's making the rounds. She'll have another uncomfortable 24 hours, but after that she should be as good as new."

"And how are Mom and Dad holding out?"

"We're exhausted, but we feel better knowing that it's nothing life-threatening."

"You did the right thing taking her into the hospital."

"I think so. By the way, I didn't forget the report you need for Mr. McMaster. I took my laptop to the hospital and got most of it done. I should be able to get down to the office in about 40 minutes, which should give me enough time to finish it."

"You're not going anywhere but to bed. I want you to e-mail me what you've done so far. You've done a great job keeping me informed on the project, so I shouldn't have any trouble filling in the blanks at this end." Chelsea laughed. "And if I don't know what's going on, I'll make something up."

"Really, Chelsea? I could —"

"I won't even allow you to consider it. Send me that e-mail and then take the rest of the day off to care for yourself and that terrific wife and baby of yours."

"Thanks, I owe you one."

ZIMCO HEAD OFFICE, NEW YORK

When Matt McMaster was appointed president and CEO of Zimco Enterprises, one of the first things he did was engage an outside firm to conduct an employee satisfaction survey. Matt, who was a corporate turnaround specialist, had long ago discovered that this was the quickest way to take the pulse of an organization. It allowed him to zero in on the main problem areas in the company.

The results of the survey he had commissioned had been delivered to him earlier that morning. The report's structure gave him an opportunity to gauge satisfaction in every area of the business and provided a comparison of results among all his division heads. The report's summary page showed him how his division managers fared against best-of-breed performers in similar industries. The results were telling.

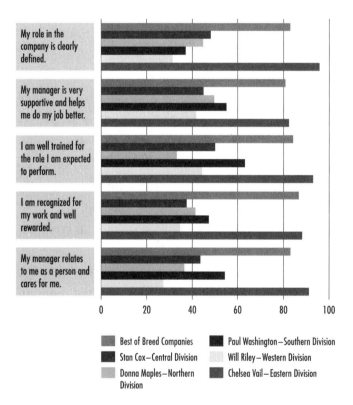

My role in the company is clearly defined.

My manager is very supportive and helps me do my job better.

I am well trained for the role I am expected to perform.

I am recognized for my work and well rewarded.

My manager relates to me as a person and cares for me.

0   20   40   60   80   100

Best of Breed Companies   Paul Washington — Southern Division
Stan Cox — Central Division   Will Riley — Western Division
Donna Maples — Northern   Chelsea Vail — Eastern Division
Division

Clearly, something extraordinary was going on in Chelsea Vail's Eastern Division that was not occurring in the rest of the company. Matt put the survey report on his desk and began tapping away on his computer keyboard. He was not surprised by the statistical profile that soon appeared on his screen. Chelsea Vail's exceptional results in the employee survey were reflected in the performance of her division. While the company was in trouble on many fronts, its problems certainly weren't reflected in Chelsea's numbers. Her team was well ahead of its business plan projections, employee turnover was minuscule, and the division was well under budget. In fact, if Chelsea's counterparts had been delivering similar performances, the board would not have felt it necessary to appoint him!

Matt logged off his PC and picked up the phone. Chelsea Vail answered her boss's call on the third ring.

"Chelsea Vail speaking, how may I help you?"

"Well, this is a nice surprise — a real live voice. I'm so used to voice mail that I'm not sure what to say," Matt chuckled. "It's Matt McMaster, Chelsea."

"Oh, hi, Matt. I think we're scheduled to meet later today."

"That's right, and I suppose I could have waited till then to talk to you, but I just had to call and congratulate you on the outstanding results you received in the employee survey."

"Well, thank you. I haven't seen the results yet."

"You'll be really pleased. In fact, if the rest of the divisions had fared as well as yours did, this company would be much stronger than it is today. I'm really anxious to know what it is you're doing that's making such a difference."

"That's easy. One simple thing — CARE."

"Care?"

"CARE."

2

Understanding CARE

Chelsea Vail had been in Matt's office for less than an hour, and already he was impressed. He listened carefully as she finished reviewing her division's performance.

Clearly the woman was as strong as the results that her business unit was turning in. Matt had refrained from asking her about CARE during her presentation, knowing that they had only a couple of hours and that it was important for Chelsea to complete her review.

"You have a good handle on the opportunities within your market and you've done a good job segmenting your customer base," Matt said.

"To be truthful, Matt, I'm just the messenger for a very strong team. I'm very fortunate. Even this presentation was prepared for me, with each of my managers contributing a section covering their respective areas of responsibility."

"I suspect you deserve some of the credit, though it's — shall I say? — 'caring' of you to give credit where credit is due."

Chelsea smiled. "I was wondering if we'd have a

chance to talk about CARE."

Matt returned her smile. "Are you kidding? It was all I could do to keep from interrupting your review to ask you about it. So, what is this CARE thing all about?"

"How long have I got?"

Matt glanced at his watch. "Probably about ten minutes. I've got another appointment at four o'clock."

"Then do you mind if we schedule another time to talk about CARE? In fact, the best thing might be for you to visit my division office, if you have the time."

"I'll make the time." Matt got out his electronic calendar. "How does the end of the week sound?"

"Friday at 9 a.m.?"

"That's perfect, Chelsea. You know you're leaving me really curious, don't you?"

"I know." She grinned. "But trust me, the full story of CARE will be worth the wait."

As part of his orientation, Matt had visited most of the floors that Zimco occupied in the building that housed its head office. But he had yet to make it to the floor where Chelsea Vail's core team worked, so his Friday morning meeting with Chelsea was going to serve a dual purpose.

As he stepped out of the elevator on the floor that housed the Eastern Division team, the first thing he noticed was the wall behind the reception area. It featured pictures of CARE award recipients. Each award seemed to have been given for excellence in a different discipline: salesperson of the month, customer caregiver of the month, support person of the month, and so on. The receptionist was on the phone when Matt arrived at the desk. He realized that she was the support person of the month — Adrienne Lacroix.

Adrienne finished her call and turned to him. "Mr. McMaster . . . I recognize you from the photo in our division newsletter. Welcome to Eastern Division."

"And I recognize you as the support person of the month. Congratulations, Adrienne. Or should I say *félicitations?*"

"*Vous parlez français?*"

"*Je parle un peu, mais quand je parle français, je pense en anglais.*"

"That's just a matter of practice. I used to think in French when I spoke English, but after about six months of working in English that doesn't happen anymore."

Matt grinned. "I'll keep working on it."

"You're here to see Chelsea, I believe. Let me show you to her office."

"Just point the way and I'll find it."

"Down the hall, first left, second right."

Chelsea's office was like the woman herself: bright and cheerful, pleasant in appearance, and modest. She and Matt exchanged niceties and then Chelsea was ready to begin discussing CARE.

"Let me tell you the story about how I discovered CARE. That's probably the best way to describe what it is."

"I'm all ears."

"Okay. Twenty-three years ago, when I was 16 —

yes, you're doing the math correctly, I am close to the big 4-0 — I attended my Grandpa Charlie's retirement party. Charlie was retiring from a company where he had worked for almost 30 years. He started as a salesman, and when he left he was one of the company's senior executives. The turnout for Charlie's party was enormous, and all I heard that night from the various guests and during the speeches was that my Grandpa Charlie was the best manager the company had ever seen. They kept referring to the CARE concept and that Charlie had not only developed the concept, he had always operated as a real CARE manager.

"To be honest, I didn't think much about that night until I got my first management job in this company, almost 16 years ago. I didn't know a thing about managing people, and there didn't appear to be a whole lot of training available that could help me, so I paid a visit to Grandpa Charlie. I asked him about CARE."

"And he introduced you to it?"

"Yeah. He was pretty shocked, mind you. I mean, the last thing he expected was to have his granddaughter asking him about something he thought had died when he left the business world."

"He must have been delighted."

"Yes, he was. He explained the CARE concept first by telling me that CARE is an acronym." Chelsea stood and moved to her office whiteboard. "This will be easier to understand if I use the board."

Matt watched as she wrote the letters of the word in a vertical line on the whiteboard:

c
a
r
E

"Why the capital E?"

"The E is larger because it represents the foundation of the CARE concept. To quote Grandpa Charlie, you could put any number of letters above the E to form whatever acronym you wanted, but without the big E, the whole thing would come tumbling down."

Chelsea wrote on the board again, starting with the letter E:

c
a
r
EMPATHY

"Empathy? Interesting. Why did Charlie believe that empathy was so important?"

"Because without empathy, without the ability to put yourself in the shoes of the people you manage, you will never know them, you certainly won't understand them, and you'll never bring them to their full potential as employees — and more important, as people."

Chelsea sat down again and continued, "Empathy is also a two-way street. As an employee, if you can't put yourself in your boss's shoes, you will never understand them and you'll never bring them to their full potential as a boss, and as a person."

"Chelsea, I agree with every word you've said. In fact, I try very much to be — to use your term — an empathetic manager. But I also believe it's because I'm an empathetic type by nature. Some aren't and never will be. It's just not in their nature."

Chelsea grinned at her boss. "You are so wrong. Give me one day with anyone you think can't be an empathetic manager or employee, and I'll turn them into one, right before your eyes."

Matt smiled and shook his head. "You can't change human nature."

"Just try me."

THE FIRST STEP TO CARE

It was obvious that Chelsea really believed in the power of CARE.

"Maybe I will," Matt said. "Why don't you finish the acronym for me and then maybe we can talk about putting CARE to the test?"

"Okay, but before we go there, you should know that there's a whole lot more behind the big E than just empathy. There's an entire training program that turns your human nature–rejects into real people."

Matt chuckled. "I'll bet there is. Just finish the acronym."

Chelsea moved back to the whiteboard. "These are pretty fundamental principles of management. They do work, however, and while empathy forms the foundation, empathy alone will not deliver the results for any organization. Following these fundamentals does."

She wrote on the board:

clear direction and support

a

r

EMPATHY

"It starts with clear direction and support. As Grandpa Charlie explained, people need to have clear direction in order to know — and then to do — what's expected of them in the job."

"I agree," Matt replied. "Direction is important."

"*Clear* direction. Too often, company executives march along thinking they're providing quality direction to their people, but if you talked to the people, you'd get all kinds of different interpretations of what the company's direction is. And there are situations where different executives are communicating different things because each has their own personal 'vision' for the company's future."

"So how have you applied clarity of direction for your division?" Matt asked.

"Every employee in our division has a one-page contract, signed by them and their manager, that stipulates what they are accountable for and what they are expected to deliver on behalf of our division and our company. These contracts are updated quarterly."

"Pretty impressive."

"I thought it was when Grandpa Charlie first told me about it."

"So these personal contracts are part of CARE?"

"The concept of the CARE contract is definitely a part of the program. Of course, they will look different for every organization, depending on the goals they've defined and the corresponding action plans they've developed in the CARE training sessions."

"Goal definition and action plan development? CARE sounds like a fairly comprehensive program."

"It is. Want to see my CARE contract?"

"You've got one, too?" Matt asked.

"Absolutely."

"Who signs yours?"

"Up until last week, your predecessor. Now I guess it's your job."

Chelsea removed a file from her desk. She opened it and took out a single page and handed it to Matt.

Matt looked at it carefully.

CHELSEA VAIL'S CARE CONTRACT — Third Quarter

What we need: Strategic Priorities

1. To achieve the division's revenue goals for third quarter, thereby ensuring that we remain in an over-achievement position relative to our year-to-date targets

2. To improve our customer satisfaction ratings from 82 to 85 percent by the end of third quarter

3. To improve our gross margin by 2 percent and reduce our

operating expense by 5 percent during the quarter, thereby increasing our division's profitability in line with published targets as identified in our business plan

4. To broaden our product and service portfolio by end of the third quarter

What addressing these needs will accomplish:
Strategic Intent

1. By achieving our revenue goals we will help our company deliver on its financial commitments to our stakeholders.
2. Higher customer satisfaction will protect our base and allow us to grow our market share accordingly, thereby assisting our company in achieving its goals.
3. By improving our profitability as a division, we will play a key role in helping the company return to profitability.
4. Timely introduction of new, targeted products and services will position us to gain competitive advantage in emerging markets.

How we will deliver to those needs: Tactical Plan

1. Grow our pending sales funnel from $225M to $250M by end of first month of third quarter; support with sales contest including monthly "blitz" days.
2. Implement customer-care call program; launch customer complaint "recovery" training.
3. Implement supply-chain integration program, thereby increasing gross margin and reducing operating expense.
4. Introduce our new Opportunity product line and our new Edge service by the end of third quarter.

By whom: Accountability for delivery
on the Tactical Plan

1. Arlene Graham, VP Sales
2. Tony Tripp, VP Customer Care
3. Stan Klein, VP Logistics
4. Sam West, VP Marketing

Strategic measures of success: Deliverables

1. Revenue of 100 percent to target in third quarter
2. Customer satisfaction at 85 percent or better by end of third quarter
3. Gross margin improvement of 2 percent and decrease in operating expense of 5 percent
4. Opportunity and Edge successfully launched

"This is great, Chelsea. And every member of your division has a personalized version of this?"

"Right."

"I can see why your division is delivering outstanding results."

"Thanks. And one thing you should know is that every division employee has access, via our local area network, to every other employee's CARE contract."

"You're kidding!"

"No, it's a critical element of the program and it speaks directly to empathy as the foundation of CARE. Think about it — why shouldn't our receptionist, for example, know what she can expect me to deliver on behalf of our division? I know what's expected of her.

And, Matt, you would be amazed what this kind of openness does for an organization. I don't have to manage or monitor anything. We have a self-monitoring business unit."

"That's brilliant!"

"That's exactly what I said to Grandpa Charlie."

"This is all part of his program?"

"Every bit of it. There's no point in defining action plans if the organization doesn't know what actions are planned, and who is accountable for delivering on those plans." Chelsea redirected Matt's attention to the whiteboard. "The *support* part of this formula is just as important, of course. And I want to reinforce that, like the *direction* component, the support that an individual can expect must also be clear."

Matt looked puzzled. "How do you make support clear?"

"Let me show you the support page of my CARE contract."

Matt grinned. "You've got a whole bunch of these, haven't you?"

"Just a few." Chelsea reached into the folder and produced another document. "This is not something that's updated quarterly. It's reviewed annually and updated, if required. It's more of a one-time agreement, between each manager and each of his or her direct reports, that ensures there is clear understanding about the support they can expect from one another. Here's the agreement I have with Sam West —"

CARE Support Contract between Chelsea Vail and Sam West

Chelsea's commitments
- I will return your calls and e-mails promptly.
- I will not create unnecessary work by micromanaging your job.
- I will allow you to make your own decisions.
- I will be available to you as a sounding board to assist you in making better decisions.
- I will assist you in the completion of your work when you need me to do so.
- I will be available to you for meetings with customers or business partners at your discretion.
- I will represent you and your initiatives fairly within the division and within the company.
- I will remain sensitive to your personal situation and respect your requirements to work often from home and to limit travel.

Sam's commitments
- I will return your calls and e-mails promptly.
- I will publicly and internally support you and your stated direction.
- I will assist you in the performance of your duties when asked.
- I will involve you in my job only when I need your experience or influence to make me more successful in mine.
- I will ensure that my personal situation does not have a negative impact on my job performance.

"Once again, I'm impressed. What's Sam's personal situation?"

"Sam's wife was killed in a car accident two years ago. He has three young children and not much family support in the vicinity. He needs the flexibility to work from home at times and it's tough for him to travel. So my commitment to him is to support him with his personal challenges. Last week, for example, I gave a speech at a conference in Atlanta that Sam was invited to deliver."

"That's really commendable."

"Well, thanks, but believe me, I get support from Sam that's five times greater than what I give to him. He's an amazing individual."

Matt was beginning to understand that Sam wasn't the only amazing individual working in Eastern Division. He had uncovered a gem in Chelsea — and in CARE.

THE SECOND STEP TO CARE

"I'll look forward to meeting Sam. What's the "A" stand for?"

Chelsea moved to the whiteboard and wrote "adequate and appropriate training."

clear direction and support
adequate and appropriate training
r
EMPATHY

"Makes sense," Matt said.

"As I indicated earlier, this is pretty fundamental stuff, but it is amazing how few organizations give training the kind of attention it deserves."

"We've always done a fair amount of training here at Zimco."

"Yes, we have . . ."

"But . . .?"

"Matt, I can only speak for my division. When I arrived here I was immediately impressed with the size of our training budget, which confirmed Zimco's commitment to training. But I was equally appalled by the inappropriate use of those training dollars."

"So, adequate funding levels but poor use of the funds."

"Precisely. The sales department is a great example. Our training dollars were being spent on large sales conferences that were very costly and delivered nothing more than nice-to-know information. We had people in the sales force who had never been taught how to qualify an account or close a deal, and we were treating them to speeches from so-called business gurus on technology trends."

"What did you do to address this?"

"Here comes Grandpa Charlie again . . ."

"Let me guess. CARE training contracts?"

"You've got it! As part of our action plan development exercise, a personal CARE training plan was prepared for every employee in our division —"

"And updated daily?"

Chelsea chuckled. "No, hourly — but you're getting the idea."

Matt smiled. "I like the play on words: *personal CARE.* Are these annual plans?"

"Exactly, and each plan is signed off by the individual and his or her manager."

"May I see yours?"

"I thought you'd never ask." Chelsea fished the document from her personal file.

Chelsea Vail's Personal CARE Training Program

1. Finance for the Non-Financial Executive — second quarter (completed)
2. ICE: Internal Consulting Expertise — third quarter
3. InterOp trade show — fourth quarter
   Budget allocation: $15,000

"These are all courses I believe I need and that your predecessor approved," Chelsea said.

"A colleague of mine took ICE, loved it, and now has his whole company being trained on the program," Matt replied.

"I've heard nothing but great things about it, so I'm anxious to take it."

"Maybe I'll join you."

"Good luck in finding a seat. ICE seminars are so

popular that they're fully booked six months in advance."

"Really? Maybe I'll bump you."

"Can't do that. I've got a signed contract."

Matt chuckled.

"I know we're just having fun here, but your joke raises a good point. Our personal CARE contracts are strictly adhered to. Nobody is allowed to skip the training for which they're scheduled unless they have their manager's approval. And, perhaps more important, no managers can bump one of their people off a course unless they have the employee's approval. Our personal CARE contracts are taken very seriously."

"I can see that," said Matt. "This whole CARE thing is really getting me thinking." He looked at the whiteboard. "How about the R in CARE?"

"Ahh . . . my favorite part, but you're going to have to wait for that one until you've treated me to lunch."

3

The Fun Part
of CARE

Lunch was superb. Chelsea discovered that, like her, Matt was into healthy eating and had an aversion for trendy, overcrowded Manhattan eateries. They grabbed a couple of bagels and some fruit and were lucky enough to find an unoccupied, sun-drenched bench in Central Park. As they ate, Chelsea learned that Matt was a father of three and that his oldest child, a girl, was planning to attend her alma mater, Duke University. Matt was pleased to hear that Chelsea had enjoyed her years at Duke.

As Matt revealed more of himself to Chelsea, she realized that he would totally relate to the final element of CARE. He was practicing quite naturally what it preached.

Once they were back at the office, Chelsea filled in the last part of the acronym, the third step to CARE:

clear direction and support
adequate and appropriate training
recognition and reward
EMPATHY

"I think this is my favorite part of CARE."

"Why's that?"

"Because it's the feel-good, fun part, and it's where I get the opportunity to acknowledge the contributions of the terrific people who comprise this division."

"That's the recognition part," Matt said, nodding his approval.

"Precisely, and thank you for understanding that. It amazes me that so many people confuse recognition and reward."

"Let me guess. They figure that if people are being well paid for what they do, that's all they need to stay motivated."

"You've got it. When I arrived here, it was widely acknowledged that the compensation plan was reasonable and that we paid our people at market levels. So, for the most part, people felt rewarded *from a compensation perspective* — and I make a distinction here — but overall, they didn't feel the company recognized their contribution as a whole or as individuals. I remember one —"

Matt interrupted, "Whoa, Chelsea. Sorry, can we just back up a moment? I want to understand this. What distinction are you making when you say that people felt rewarded from a compensation perspective?"

"They felt that their salaries and bonuses were fair."

"But . . . ?"

"They didn't feel that they were being rewarded for their actual contributions."

Matt looked puzzled. "I'm confused."

"Let me give you an example. When I arrived here, our customer service representatives — whom we now refer to as customer CARE reps, by the way — were paid a little above the industry standard. They also had a bonus plan that gave them an opportunity to earn an additional 20 percent of their base salary. This was an excellent compensation plan and the people acknowledged it. What the plan didn't do, however, was truly reward them for good performance. Their bonus plan, for example, was based on how quickly they could handle customer calls."

"I take it they're on the phone all day."

"Right, they man the phones in C-cubed —"

"C-cubed?"

"Oh, sorry, our Customer CARE Center — CCC?"

"Got it."

"Anyway, our CARE reps were paid based on speed of call handling instead of quality of care given."

"As measured by our customer satisfaction survey results."

"Exactly," said Chelsea. "We changed the bonus plan and started rewarding them for what they are really accountable for delivering —"

"Let me guess. The results went through the roof!"

"In a heartbeat. And we made sure that there was a real upside to the bonus plan. Since better customer service paved the way for us to achieve higher market share and strong revenue growth, we put some extra rewards in place, based not only on achievement of customer satisfaction goals, but also on realizing our revenue and share goals."

"Was this across all departments in your division?" Matt asked.

"Right."

"So each department benefits in some way when another department achieves its goals."

Chelsea nodded. "Exactly, and our employee survey results confirm that our people feel rewarded for the quality of their work — not just for how many calls they take or orders they process."

"That's great." Matt paused for a moment. "We kind of slipped past the *recognition* part of CARE. Is there more you can share with me about recognition?"

"Sure. The fundamental belief underlying the recognition element of CARE is that *recognizing* people for what they contribute is just as important as *rewarding* them. Recognition should be done publicly, and shouldn't come only from on high."

"Can you illustrate this?"

"Sure. Our recognition program issues CARE shares as an acknowledgement of outstanding contribution."

"CARE shares?"

Chelsea pointed to the wall behind Matt. "*CARE shares.*" Matt turned to look at the wall.

"Very nice." Matt turned to face Chelsea. "What did you do?"

"Not a lot, trust me. I think a collective guilt was building up because I was one of the few people in the division who had never received a CARE share."

CARE *Shares*

Issued to: Chelsea Vail
By: Morgan Shirley,
Director of Sales, Northeast Area
In recognition of: Assistance in
closing Conrad deal
Share value: 100 units

"What does a CARE share entitle one to?"

"Before I answer that, remember that this is primarily a recognition program. It's administered by a group consisting of employee representatives from each department. This team accepts recommendations for CARE share recognition from any employee in the division. We issue 1,000 CARE shares every month and this committee determines who gets them."

"So it's not run by management."

"Managers are part of it, but it's not a top-down recognition program, if that's what you mean. When a person receives an award, he or she becomes part of the CARE share recognition committee, replacing the representative from his or her particular department."

"I really like this," Matt said. "The people must feel so involved."

"They really do. In fact, the team designed the program in response to the recognition action plans we developed in our very first CARE training session."

"Interesting. I noticed the share-value component. So what do the shares entitle one to?"

"Not much. We have a prize catalog provided by a local company. Each share is valued at two dollars, and the maximum share issue to an individual at one time is 200. The minimum is 50."

"So each recognition award is worth between $100 and $400."

"Right."

"This is very impressive."

"Want to be even more impressed?" Chelsea didn't wait for Matt to reply. "This program has been in place for over a year. We've awarded CARE shares valued at a total of $30,000 to more than a hundred members of this division, and not one person has cashed in a share — not one."

"You've got to be kidding."

"No. I suppose they will at some point in time, but for now, the share certificates are hanging in offices and on baffles everywhere. They have become an immense source of pride for their owners, and they're serving as a very visible symbol of excellent performance. The share-owners don't want to give them up. And believe me, the people who haven't earned one are working even harder in pursuit of recognition from their peers."

"So the recognition for their excellent work is more important than the money," Matt concluded.

"Exactly."

"Chelsea, I can see why your division is delivering such outstanding results. You are clearly providing strong leadership. I am delighted to have you as a member of my team."

"Thank you so much, Matt."

"You're very welcome. Now, having said that, I'd really like to take you up on your offer."

"What offer?"

"How did you put it? 'Try me'? I'd like you to help me implement CARE across all our divisions. Quite frankly, this company is in trouble. Confidentially, my job is to turn the company around — or to close it down."

"Close the company?"

"Our parent corporation is not happy with our performance. My mandate is clear. I either turn it around in one year, or make the call to close a money-losing company. I think CARE can help me achieve that turn-around."

"Matt, I know it can, but I'm not sure I'd be comfortable among my peers being set up as the white knight."

"Chelsea, I need —"

"Matt, I'm not saying we can't deploy CARE throughout the company. I'm just saying that I'm not the person to make it happen."

"If not you, then who?"

Chelsea grinned. "That's a no-brainer — my Grandpa Charlie!"

"Your grandfather is still alive?"

"And kicking."

"Wow . . . Well, how old a man is he?"

"He'll be 79 on his next birthday."

"Chelsea, I'm sure your grandfather was a very capable man during his prime but —"

"Matt, how old was Ronald Reagan when he served as president of the United States?"

Now it was Matt's turn to blush. "Okay, you've made your point. I take it your Grandpa Charlie has all his faculties."

"Charlie will challenge you like nobody you've ever met."

"Then I can't wait to meet him."

Chelsea called her grandfather on his cellular phone shortly after Matt left her office. Charlie Woods answered her call on the first ring.

"G'day, it's Charlie here."

"G'day yourself!"

"Oh, no . . . It can't be . . . Could it be? Is this my long-lost granddaughter?"

"Very funny. It's only been two weeks since we talked."

"And a good two months since I've seen you."

"A month and a half — on my birthday, or don't you remember?"

"I remember that you used to have time for your Grandpa until you got that high-and-mighty job of yours."

Chelsea laughed. "Charlie darling, you will never change. How are you?"

"I couldn't be better! The sun's shining, I met the girl of my dreams last night, and I shot my age for the third time this summer."

"That's fantastic!"

"Yeah, she's a real doll!"

Chelsea laughed again. "I meant the golf. Hasn't anybody told you that you're getting a little long in the tooth to be chasing the girls? Given your behavior, it's amazing Grandma isn't haunting you."

"She only haunts me on the golf course. I blame her for all my three-putts."

They were quiet for a moment, remembering the woman they had both loved so dearly. She had passed away over five years ago, and it had taken Charlie a good two years to start living again. Charlie always teased Chelsea about the women in his life, but there was only one woman who would ever be part of him — his beloved Ivy.

Chelsea broke the silence. "Charlie, you sound like you're in a tunnel. Where are you?"

"I'm in my car. I've got you on the hands-free unit."

"Oh, that explains it."

"So, what's up? You wouldn't be calling me in the middle of the day unless you wanted something, so lay it on me."

"Charlie, I don't *want* anything. I do *need* you though, or more accurately, my company needs you."

"Let me guess. CARE?"

"How did you know?"

"The only time we ever talk about business is when we discuss CARE, though there's nothing wrong with that."

"You know the success I've had with CARE. My company, however, hasn't fared so well. My division is the only profitable one in Zimco, and if we don't turn things around quickly, I'm afraid the company could go under. I know CARE can make a difference. And I know you're the only person who can implement CARE in the time frame we need. Are you interested?"

"Maybe . . ." Charlie paused to collect his thoughts. "I read that you've got a new president. Is he aware of this?"

"Matt McMaster — he's aware and he's completely supportive. He understands the value of CARE, and he's anxious to implement the concept throughout the company."

"Hmmm . . . He's not one of those snot-nosed, arrogant, academic business-school types, is he? I don't think I have the patience to deal with any more of those."

Chelsea chuckled, remembering Charlie's most recent consulting experience. He had succeeded in implementing the CARE concept, but maintained that he had had to put half the management team "over his knee" to make it happen.

"No, he's well educated, I'm sure, like your granddaughter," Chelsea said, "but he's learned through experience and he's a real feet-on-the-ground kind of guy."

"Any biases?"

"Well, he's not so sure that people can really change."

"I can deal with that. Does he know how old I am?"

"I gave him the Ronald Reagan line."

"Worked like a charm, did it?"

"Yup."

"Okay, I'll meet with him. McMaster, you said?"

"Right, Matt McMaster. Thank you, Charlie. I love you."

"I love you, too, dear. Get him to give me a call and we'll see what we can do."

Meeting Grandpa Charlie

It had been almost a week since Charlie agreed to meet his granddaughter's boss. He was delighted when Matt McMaster agreed to his suggestion that they get to know one another over a round of golf. Charlie had always found that five hours on the golf course was a great way to start a relationship with a business associate.

He drove into the parking lot of Tiger Claw, Matt McMaster's golf club, and pulled up near the entrance. Charlie stepped out of his Saab as a young lad removed his golf bag.

"Good morning, sir. Looks like you're going to have a beautiful day to play."

"I think you're right. But then, there's no such thing as a bad day for golf."

The young man smiled. "You got that right."

"I'm playing with Matt McMaster. Do you know him?"

The attendant pointed to the putting green next to the clubhouse. "That's him right there: the tall, blond gentleman in the khaki pants and the black-and-tan shirt."

Charlie looked toward the practice green. "Thanks," he said. Matt McMaster looked fit. Charlie liked that; it implied a disciplined lifestyle.

The young man offered to park the car for him. Charlie accepted and walked over to the putting green. "Mr. McMaster."

Matt looked up to see a tall, gray-haired, distinguished-looking gentleman dressed entirely in black. Charlie Woods looked much as Matt had imagined from Chelsea's description.

"Mr. Woods, nice to meet you, and please call me Matt." They shook hands.

"And I'm Charlie. And given your youth, the extra practice you're getting here, and this being your home course, I expect you'll be giving me strokes today."

Matt smiled warmly. "In your dreams. Chelsea told me about your game."

"Ahh, I never liked that girl . . ."

Matt McMaster lined up his putt. If he sank it, he would shoot a 78 and beat Charlie by a single stroke. Matt tapped the ball and watched it roll ten feet and drop squarely in the hole.

"Yes!" he exclaimed, pumping his fist.

"You dog!" Charlie shouted.

Matt laughed. "Hey, did you think I was going to let an old lad like you beat me? No way!"

Charlie smiled and shook Matt's hand. He liked

Chelsea's boss. He was an honest, friendly man with a real competitive spirit.

They proceeded to the clubhouse, which was as impressive as the course itself. While a relatively new club, Tiger Claw had managed to create an environment that exuded a certain old-world charm. After settling into comfortable leather chairs overlooking the eighteenth green and ordering sandwiches and beer, both men were ready to get down to business. It was finally time to talk about CARE.

"Charlie, I think Chelsea has told you about our situation."

"She did, yes, though I suspect you can give me a broader perspective."

"I hope so," said Matt. "Zimco is in trouble, I think you know that. I've been given three months to assess the situation and bring a recommendation to our board. The expectation is that I will deliver either a turnaround strategy or a wind-down strategy — nothing in between."

"I've read about some of the problems you've been having. Continuing to limp along as you have for the last few years is certainly not an option."

"No." Matt frowned, leaving no doubt in Charlie's mind about what the future could hold for Zimco and for his granddaughter.

"Matt, let me tell you right now that CARE can help you effect a turnaround. I'll be honest and tell you it's not the answer to all your problems, but if your strategy is sound, it will allow you to deliver on that strategy."

"The right strategy is not a problem. It's the execution that concerns me. I'm just not sure I have the right team under me, and I don't have the luxury of time to turn things around gradually."

"Matt, rest assured you have the right people. All they need is CARE. This is not a quick fix, mind you. The components of CARE are easy enough to understand, but unless they are implemented on the right foundation, all the training in the world won't help your situation."

"You're referring to the *empathy* component of CARE?"

"That's right. And acquiring the ability to empathize takes time — time and effort."

"I guess that's the part that concerns me. Can people really learn how to empathize?"

"Ahh, the human nature element."

"Yeah . . ."

"A lot of people believe that a person's nature can't change, and I suppose I fundamentally agree with that. However, I also believe that nobody's nature is such that they want to be a rotten boss or a rotten employee. They just don't know how to change. They don't know how to empathize. CARE training teaches them that skill."

Matt nodded.

"And once an organization is CARE-enabled," Charlie went on, "I guarantee that you will start to see a tremendous increase in shareholder value."

"That's a pretty bold statement."

"Matt, I'm too old to make bold statements unless I can back them up. At my age, everything I tell you is

based on fact. Here, I want to show you something."
Charlie reached into his pocket and pulled out a sheet of
paper. He unfolded it and laid it out on the table for Matt
to see.

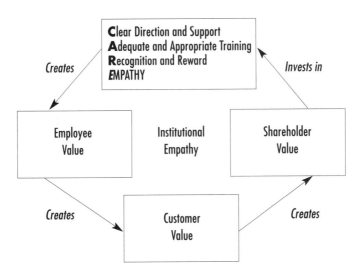

"Matt, are you familiar with those recent studies that
attempted to quantify employee value, and then looked
at that value in terms of its impact on the company's
market value?"

"Vaguely."

"It's pretty interesting stuff." Charlie pointed to the
diagram. "Essentially, the studies concluded that
increasing employee value — or employee satisfaction, if
you prefer — will increase customer value, that is, your
customers' perception of your value in the marketplace.
This in turn will increase shareholder value. The
missing part of this equation, however, is how does one
increase employee value? The answer is with CARE."

Matt examined the chart as Charlie spoke. "Let me get this straight. If my employees place a high value on being employed by Zimco, they will be happy and motivated."

"You will have high employee value," Charlie confirmed.

"Okay. The employees, in turn, will represent Zimco in the marketplace in a manner that will increase Zimco's value in the eyes of our customers."

"Right, you will have a higher customer valuation. In other words, your customers will value your products and services more than they value them today. And since customer value is defined in relation to how your competitors are valued, achieving a higher customer value rating automatically means that you have gained value relative to your competitors."

"We've improved our competitive position."

"Right."

"Okay, higher customer value means more business for Zimco, which in turn will create higher shareholder value."

"You've got it."

"It seems so simple."

"It is simple, which is why CARE is such an effective program."

Matt liked what he was hearing, and he certainly had proof of the power of CARE in Chelsea's division. He was also very impressed by the older man who sat across from him.

"Charlie, how long will it take to implement CARE?"

"You have four divisions that need help?"

"Right, and each division has roughly 400 people."

"The size of the organization doesn't matter. We start at the top and, once your senior people are operating as CARE managers, the rest of the company will pick it up in a matter of weeks." Charlie paused, deep in thought. "I can make this happen for you in eight weeks — two for each division."

"Then you've got yourself a deal."

5

The Path
to Empathy

ZIMCO WESTERN DIVISION, LOS ANGELES

Will Riley wasn't particularly happy. He had spent the better part of the morning listening to this old guy talk about his CARE system, and that was fine. The ideas about direction, training, reward, and recognition made a whole lot of sense. He just didn't understand why it was necessary for this old geezer to spend every minute of every day with him. The guy had been waiting for him when he'd arrived at work, had attended the boss's weekly video conference, and had followed him right back to his office. From behind his big oak desk, Will looked directly at Charlie, who was sitting quietly on the office couch. They hadn't said one word to each other since they'd left Matt's meeting more than 20 minutes ago. Finally, Will broke the silence.

"So, Charlie, let me understand this. You're supposed to spend the next two days with me while I do my job. Is that correct?"

"That's right, Will."

"So even when I visit the john, you'll be with me?"

"That depends."

"Oh, really? On what?"

"On whether or not you're working in the john."

Will exhaled loudly and shook his head in disbelief. "Whatever . . ." He activated his hands-free phone and punched a number on the speed-dialer.

Molly Shannon answered on the second ring, "Hi, it's Molly. May I help you?"

"Molly, Will. Bailey tells me you're not able to attend our meeting this afternoon."

"That's right, Will. Sorry, I have to take Liam to —"

"Molly!" Will interrupted. "I don't care what your excuse is. Attendance at my meetings is mandatory. You know that."

"Will, I haven't missed a meeting in a year. I was going to send Ralph to represent —"

"No delegates. You know that, too. I'll see you at 1:00 sharp." Riley hung up the phone before Molly could answer. As he did so, he glanced quickly at Charlie Woods. The old man's expression hadn't changed all morning. *God, this was annoying. What could Matt McMaster be thinking?*

Each division at Zimco operated as a profit-and-loss entity with end-to-end responsibility for one of Zimco's product lines. As such, the divisions were completely autonomous entities, affording the division managers a tremendous amount of power and control.

Charlie scanned the meeting room, registering the names of the attendees and their respective functions:

Oscar Long, VP Marketing and Sales; Veronica Brown, VP Operations; Tony Hale, VP Human Resources and Administration; Bailey Stevens, Will's personal assistant; and Molly Shannon, Customer Service, whose attendance confirmed that Riley's intimidation tactics had worked.

Will Riley was at the head of the table. "Oscar, you're up."

Oscar Long rose and moved to the end of the boardroom table. He slid an overhead onto the projector and flipped on the unit. Charlie examined the graph carefully. It did not present a pretty picture.

Riley let out a sigh. "This is dismal, Oscar! You keep telling me sales are picking up. So why am I not seeing these so-called new sales reflected in your results?"

"We've sold more than is reflected in our financials. Our problem is that we haven't been able to implement much of what we've sold." Oscar looked at Veronica Brown. "Sorry, Veronica, but your team just isn't delivering what we're promising to our customers."

"Maybe we wouldn't have this problem if your salespeople weren't selling services we don't offer!" Veronica's expression did nothing to hide her anger.

Oscar, suddenly red-faced, raised his voice in reply, "That, my dear, is called customization! The sooner you understand that we have to be able to customize our solutions to win business in today's world, the better off we're going to be!"

Riley tapped his water glass repeatedly with his pen to regain control of the meeting. "That's enough! Oscar, your results stink. Fix them fast or think about another career. Veronica, step up to the plate and start implementing on time or you can join your friend here on the unemployment line! DO I MAKE MYSELF CLEAR?"

Charlie watched in amazement as the two combatants responded to Will's threats with bowed heads and an uncomfortable silence. In all his years in the business world, he had never seen anything quite like this. Will Riley was the classic schoolyard bully. Charlie recalled the employee survey information he'd reviewed in preparation for the training exercise with Riley and his senior team. Morale within the division was incredibly low. Employee turnover was ridiculously high. It was no wonder, then, that Riley's division's results were so poor.

Charlie looked at Riley, who was now berating Bailey Stevens in an effort to reduce the division's receivables. He took a deep breath and let it out slowly. Charlie believed in the power of CARE, but he now realized that the system was about to be put to its ultimate challenge. Could CARE turn this sinking ship around? A lot depended on his ability to get to Riley. He knew how to do it; he just wasn't sure he could convince Matt McMaster to do what had to be done.

Charlie's flight from Los Angeles to New York gave him time to address the challenge he was facing with Will Riley. By the time he met with Matt McMaster, he had formulated a plan of action.

As Charlie described in great detail what had transpired at Will Riley's meeting, Matt hung on every word.

"This is unbelievable," Matt said.

"I was pretty overwhelmed by the whole thing."

"I know Will's a pretty demanding guy, but I had no idea that he was abusive to his people."

"Probably the worst part is that the abuse doesn't stop with his own people. Quite frankly, the man terrorizes the entire company. I spent the better part of the afternoon after the meeting chatting with people outside Will's division. It's pretty apparent that they're all very intimidated by Mr. Riley."

Matt looked skyward, searching for inspiration. "It's a damned shame, you know. Riley is a brilliant guy. He's a terrific strategist. He really knows our industry and has an incredible network of contacts. He's probably the most hard-nosed negotiator I've ever worked with, too."

After another deep sigh, Matt continued, "I guess I have no choice but to fire him."

"No, Matt, what he needs is CARE. Only, in his case, maybe a more dramatic version of the system needs to be applied."

"You think he's salvageable?"

"Maybe, maybe not. But it's certainly worth the effort to try. From what I can see, Will does have a strong managerial skill set. It appears that he knows the importance of the C-A-R steps of CARE. He's determined to deliver clear direction and support, adequate and appropriate training, and recognition and reward. He just doesn't have the requisite people skills to make those things happen."

"The empathy foundation is missing."

"Precisely."

"So, what needs to be done?

"Matt, did you ever encounter a schoolyard bully when you were a young lad?"

Matt laughed. "Oh, did I ever. There was one kid who bullied me and most of my friends for the better part of my freshman year in high school. He was a big, heavy sophomore who gave me more than one good pounding. Brian Bain — I hated that kid."

"Did he bully you all through high school?"

"No, the bullying stopped rather abruptly during the first week of my sophomore year."

"What happened?"

Matt smiled. "We had been back to school for a couple of days when Bain made the mistake of picking on a new kid, Sloan Slater, who had just moved to our district. Sloan was a fairly small kid. Bain was almost a head taller than he, and must have outweighed him by 50 pounds. What Bain didn't know, however, was that Sloan had a black belt in karate. The reason the Slaters moved to our city was to let Sloan train with a former world karate champion.

"Bain deliberately bumped Sloan in the schoolyard one day, knocking his books all over the place. When Sloan bent to pick them up, Bain knocked him off balance with his foot. Sloan didn't respond and tried again to pick up his books. Bain made a move to push him off balance one more time. That was his last attempt at bullying that anybody ever saw. Sloan destroyed him. He kicked Bain's legs out from underneath him and, when Bain went after him again, Sloan methodically reduced this big lug to tears in front of half the student population." It was clear that Matt was relishing the memory. "It was beautiful."

"And the bully never bothered anybody ever again?" Charlie asked.

"He never did. In fact, he became a gentle giant, and by his senior year was considered one of the nicer guys in the school." Matt smiled. "I see where you're leading me here."

"I thought that you would."

"So what do we do?"

"Bully the bully . . ."

The morning after his meeting with Matt, Charlie was pleased that Chelsea could join him for breakfast at his favorite Manhattan deli. Chelsea knew the CARE system as well as he did, and he really needed to bounce his plan for Riley off somebody who thoroughly understood CARE.

"I heard that things were pretty bad in Will's division, but I had no idea they were that bad. It sounds like a real reign of terror."

"That's a good way to describe it." Charlie paused, then looked directly at Chelsea. "You know Riley. What do you think of my plan?"

"Well, it's risky. But if you don't get through to him,

he's never going to agree to the role plays, and the role plays are an essential part of CARE training. I don't think you have any other options."

"That's more or less what I concluded. I'm glad you agree."

"How are you going to set it up?"

"Matt is going to call Riley to a meeting here in New York. When he gets there, I'll be there and so will all his direct reports. Riley will not know the purpose of the meeting. When he arrives, Matt is going to destroy the bully."

"Ouch . . . But Matt's such a warm, caring guy. Do you think he can do this?"

Charlie laughed. "We had a little coaching session last evening. It'll be a stretch, but he knows what to do and I think he'll be effective."

"Do you think it'll work?"

"We'll find out soon enough." Charlie looked at his watch. "The show begins about an hour from now."

The look on Will Riley's face made it clear that he was shocked to see his entire Los Angeles team sitting in the boardroom that adjoined his boss's office. He glanced at Charlie, his disdain for the man obvious.

"What's up?"

Charlie looked at the members of Will's team. They had been briefed on the purpose of the meeting and understood that their role was to be passive observers. This was Matt's show. Nobody was to step forward in an effort to rescue the bully.

Matt spoke without warmth, "Sit down, Will."

Will sat, a puzzled expression on his face. "Okay."

From his place at the head of the table, Matt said, "What the hell is going on with your results? You promised double-digit growth this quarter and you're —"

"Matt, I —"

"DON'T INTERRUPT ME WHEN I'M SPEAKING! I'm already having to make excuses to the board for the dismal performance of your division. Your staff turnover is the highest in the company, morale is incredibly low, your . . ."

As Matt hammered away at Riley, Charlie carefully watched the group dynamics of the room. The discomfort that the members of Riley's team were feeling was evident. Jaws were clenched, arms were folded, and faces were flushed — none more so than Riley's, which was beet red. The man was clearly very angry. As Matt piled on the criticism, Riley's head began to bow in humiliation at the treatment he was receiving. As they had been instructed, Riley's direct reports stared at their boss, although the team's discomfort was palpable.

It was time for Charlie to step in. He stood up as he spoke. "Matt, thank you. I think we've heard enough."

Will Riley looked up. "What the —"

"Will, this has been a staged bullying, I guess you could call it."

"Matt, I don't understand . . ."

In a gentler tone, Matt said, "Just listen, Will, please."

Charlie continued, "Will, you are a very bright man and you have good intentions. There's not a person in this room who does not respect your ability. The sad reality, however, is that you are a bully. You intimidate your team members. You intimidate the employees of your division. You make Western Division a horrible place to work; people leave the division solely because of you. You have trouble attracting top talent because of your reputation."

Charlie paused to let his harsh words sink in. He looked closely at Will, whose expression told him what he needed to know: they had reached him in a meaningful way. "You need to change — and the CARE concept will help you do that, if you embrace it."

Will looked around the room, his eyes settling in turn on each of its occupants. "I . . . I'm sorry . . . I had no idea that you . . . Do I really come across as badly as" — he laughed nervously — "as the boss here?"

Molly answered on behalf of the team, "Will, as Charlie said, we respect your ability, and outside the office you are an okay guy. But you intimidate the heck out of all of us. You make us feel exactly the way Matt made you feel today."

The others nodded in agreement.

"Wow." He shook his head in disbelief. "This is a . . . rude awakening." He looked at Charlie. "I guess I've got you to thank for the wake-up call. Where do we go from here?"

"Thank you, Will. You've already taken a big step

forward in turning your division around. We start taking the next steps the day after tomorrow." Charlie scanned the room. "Ladies, gentlemen, put on your acting shoes, because you're about to experience the foundation of CARE."

Learning to
Empathize

The trip home to Los Angeles gave Will Riley a lot of time to think about how he had felt when faced with the verbal assault dished out by his boss. More important, it gave him time to reflect on his own managerial style. While Will wasn't exactly a changed man, he was certainly now very open to change.

That reality was clear to every member of Will's team, and to Charlie, when the team reconvened at the Los Angeles offices of Zimco.

"So the exercise the day before yesterday was actually part of CARE?" Will asked Charlie.

"A rather dramatic part, but yes, it was part of the program. Or maybe, more accurately, it's a technique used within CARE to facilitate the development of empathy. It's nothing new, but I'm afraid it's not used a whole lot these days. It's called the role play."

"Isn't a role play very staged?" Will asked.

"Yes, Will, it is. And so was yesterday's session. Every person in the room, you excepted, knew the role they were expected to play."

Will laughed. "So you guys ganged up on me?"

There was nervous laughter from the occupants of the boardroom. It was clear to Charlie that they had not yet bought into the notion of a "new and improved" Will Riley. That would take a little time.

"That's right, Will," Charlie said. "We got together in advance and set up a role play, which allowed us to illustrate a point."

"Interesting . . ."

"And now we're going to undertake a series of role plays designed to help us learn a little more about each other and the pressures each of us faces."

Charlie patted a thick black binder that he had brought to the meeting. "This here's my empathy bible. I've collected role-play situations over the years and made a catalog of them according to circumstances that we're trying to address."

"How do you use them, exactly?" Molly Shannon asked.

"The role plays are tailored to each person's real circumstances. For example, based on the conversation you and I had yesterday, I know some things about you, and what you deal with on a daily basis, that your boss isn't aware of. Conversely, I know some things about Will and what he deals with day to day that you are not privy to. So I have selected a role play for the two of you to perform."

"Charlie, can you elaborate on what it is we are trying to accomplish here?" Bailey Stevens asked.

"Of course, Bailey. We're going to teach each of you a

little about what it's like to walk in the other guy's shoes. Once you've learned that, you'll find it easier to relate to each other and, more important, you'll have developed an empathy for each other that you've never experienced before."

"Does this really work?" Will asked. "I mean, how can Molly feel what I feel, or vice versa?"

Charlie smiled. "Watch and learn." He opened his binder and pulled out a role-play document. "Normally I'd have spent a little more time designing a tailored role play for the two of you, but due to time constraints, I don't have that luxury."

Charlie handed a single document each to Molly and Will, and gave copies of both documents to the other occupants of the room. "Take a few moments to read what I've given you, and then we'll get the show on the road. By the way, Molly is playing the role of Martha Carter and Will is her assistant, Arnold Delano."

"Arnold? Couldn't you have given me a better name?" Will said.

"Martha isn't exactly one of my favorites either," Molly added.

Charlie waited until the friendly banter and chuckles subsided. "Okay, Will and Molly, remember that you are going to be acting out the situation described in these documents, so pay close attention to the background details I've given you. The rest of you people are going to be observers, but you will be asked to provide feedback at the end of the role play. So read away."

Role Play #1
Molly in the role of "Martha"

You manage a group of ten clerks or, as you like to call them, "support staff." You've been with the company for ten years, six of which you have spent as a manager. As a manager, you have always had staff reporting to you, and you like that. You enjoy coaching, training, and managing your people; you take pride in seeing them develop professionally. You remember all their birthdays, usually sense when one of them has a problem, and encourage them to come to you "about anything."

Lately there have been significant budget cuts in your organization and you've even heard rumors of layoffs. Your no-nonsense boss, who is under a lot of pressure, has been warning you that the situation is serious, and that if the productivity of your clerical unit doesn't improve, your team will likely be the first group affected. Also, there is to be no overtime and absolutely no travel, and you'd better toe the line on expenses. Even more worrisome to you, any person who appears to be not very busy (i.e., redundant) had better worry about job security. The story you've heard is that the layoffs will start with non-management staff, so you're worried about your people.

This morning you arrive as usual at 8:30. Your senior clerk, Arnold, who is supposed to start at 8:00, is not in yet; his desk is still locked. This is the fifth time in two weeks that Arnold has been late. Although you are not at liberty to tell him about the dire situation in the company, you have warned him about his tardiness.

Your boss, looking very stressed, passes, and looks

at Arnold's desk. He raises his eyebrows at you and continues on his way. You know he expects you to do something about Arnold as soon as he arrives, which he does a few minutes later. With years of supervisory training behind you, you wisely decide to wait until you are better prepared to speak with Arnold, so you ask him to see you at 10:00. This will also give you time to complete the staff reduction impact report your boss is waiting for.

You return to your office and begin to work on the report, only to have your thinking process interrupted by a conversation just outside between Arnold and another member of your staff. While you can't make out everything they are saying, it's obvious that the discussion is not work-related. In fact, Arnold hasn't even unlocked his desk yet! After ten minutes you can't take any more, so you approach Arnold . . .

Will in the role of "Arnold"

You are a hard-working, dedicated clerk with over five years of company service. You've been in your present job for two years, and it appears that your hard work is finally starting to pay off. Your boss, with whom you get along quite well, has recently given you a "promotable" rating. Several months ago she indicated she was looking for opportunities to promote you into a management position. However, while things are going well on the job front, the opposite is true at home.

Your marriage is in trouble, and your wife has threatened to leave you — and your four-year-old son. While you have come to realize that the marriage is probably not worth saving, you are very concerned about the financial problems associated with raising a young child on a clerk's salary. You tend to keep your personal problems to yourself, so no one in the office knows about this.

You and your wife have been arguing a lot lately, usually in the morning when you're trying to get ready for work (she works nights). This particular morning, after an especially nasty confrontation, you and your wife finally decided to call it quits. Your little boy overheard the whole thing, which has really upset both him and you. Taking time to calm him down and assure him that everything is going to be all right has made you late for work (again!). You're so stressed out that you're pouring out your troubles to a co-worker when Martha approaches you . . .

Charlie looked around the room. "Everybody all done?"

The members of the group nodded in unison. Charlie looked at Molly and smiled. "Okay, we're almost ready to start." He reached into his briefcase and extracted a handful of buzzers, which he passed out to each of the room's occupants. "Please use these sparingly. If, however, you see behavior from either of our role players that you feel is not appropriate, buzz them and we'll stop the role play to hear your comments."

"This is going to be fun," said Bailey as she pressed the buzzer.

Her peers laughed and hit their buzzers in response.

"Okay, children," a smiling Charlie replied, "just

remember, you'll be going through one of these role plays as well, so be kind."

Oscar buzzed a response. "No problem. Bring it on!"

Charlie couldn't resist a chuckle. "Okay, Martha," he said to Molly, "let's go."

"So I . . ."

"Act out the scene. You are a manager in this company who is faced with a dilemma. Handle it."

"Okay," Molly replied, her anxiety evident.

Martha approaches Arnold, who is chatting away to one of his colleagues. He doesn't notice her arrival on the scene.

"Arnold, excuse me, but it's almost nine o'clock. This is the third time this week you've been late. This has got to stop! Consider this a final —"

Veronica Brown depressed her buzzer.

Charlie turned toward her. "Veronica?"

"Reprimand in private, praise in public."

"Good point." Charlie looked at the role-players. "Arnold, when Martha approached you the way she did, how did it make you feel?"

"Embarrassed. I didn't like being criticized in front of my peers."

"Did any other emotions surface?"

"I guess it made me a little angry."

"How did it make you feel about your boss?"

"I certainly didn't respect her for it."

Charlie looked at Molly. "Molly, have you ever been on the receiving end of this kind of interaction?"

Molly looked down, clearly reluctant to reply.

Charlie urged a response, "We're here to learn the foundation of CARE, remember?"

She looked up. "All the time. I'm constantly being embarrassed by being criticized publicly."

"And do you deserve to be criticized?" Charlie asked.

"Yes, sometimes I do, I admit that. But often there are extenuating circumstances that make the criticism unfair."

"Ahh, the good old 'extenuating circumstance.' Excellent. Let's move on."

"Back to the role play?" asked Will.

"Yes, and since we had only just started, how about taking it from the top?"

Martha approaches Arnold, who is chatting away to one of his colleagues. He doesn't notice her arrival on the scene.

"Excuse me, Arnold, can I see you for a moment?" Martha asks.

"Oh . . . sure." Arnold turns to his peer. "I'll fill you in on the rest of it later."

Martha walks to her 'office' and Arnold follows her. She takes her seat behind her desk and Arnold sits in the low chair in front of it.

"Arnold, this is the third time this week you have been late. This has got to stop. Things are not good around here right now, and if you don't shape up and start getting here on time, you are not going to be an employee of Zimco much longer."

This time, the buzzer was pressed by Charlie. "Okay, let's stop here for a minute," he said. "Any comments or observations from you guys?" He looked around the room.

"I'm not a big fan of the power-seating arrangement," Tony Hale volunteered. "Regardless of the message that's being delivered, I feel that Martha should have sat at the round table beside her desk and invited Arnold to join her."

"Arnold? What do you have to say about it?"

"Sitting in that low chair in front of Martha's desk made me feel like a schoolboy being reprimanded for something I'd done wrong."

"Anything else?"

He sheepishly replied, "I . . . I always sit in the power position. I guess I thought it made me more . . ."

"Intimidating?"

"I never thought about it in those terms, but I suppose so."

"Remember, real power comes from gaining the respect and admiration of others. It never derives from the title beside your name or from where you sit." Charlie paused to let the implications of what he had just said sink in. After a moment, he continued, "Anything else?"

The room was silent, so Charlie volunteered his observation, "Martha has not made any effort to get to the root cause of Arnold's behavior. As your role-play description sheets indicate, Arnold is a really good employee. He's got a promotable rating and he's well regarded by his boss. The behavior that Martha is

seeing from Arnold is very uncharacteristic. What does
that tell us?"

Oscar Lang replied, "There's something else going on
here. Right, Martha?"

She nodded in agreement. "I guess I'd better find
out."

Martha looks across the desk at Arnold. "Why don't we sit
over here at the round table?"

"That would be a little more comfortable. Thank you."

Once seated, Martha softly states, "Arnold, you are an
excellent employee, one of the top people in our unit.
And you know I've recently recommended you for a
promotion."

"I know that, Martha, and I'm thankful. I could really
use the extra money."

"The problem right now, Arnold, is that your behavior
in the last couple of weeks is totally inconsistent with that
of a top performer. You've been late for work several
times and, quite frankly, when you are here, you seem
totally detached from your work."

"I know. I . . ." Arnold avoids his boss's gaze. "I've . . .
I've had a few personal problems that I guess I'm not
handling very well."

"My God, Arnold, why didn't you tell me? Is there anything I can do to help?"

Charlie interrupted the role play with a buzz. "This is
beautiful. What we're witnessing here is Martha reaching

out to Arnold in a very empathetic way. Her warmth and sincerity are evident, and as a result she is getting to the root cause of the problem. Please continue."

"Well, my wife's a real witch, Martha. Maybe you could fix me up with Cindy Crawford?"

The room exploded with laughter. *This is good,* Charlie thought. *When humor creeps into the role plays it's a sign that real team bonding is starting to occur.*
"Let's try again, kiddies."

Arnold continues, "I'm having a tough time on the home front right now. My wife and I are separating and we'll be getting a divorce. We're not apart yet and it seems that all we do is fight. That's why I've been late so often. She gets home from the hospital just before I'm supposed to leave for work, and. the fighting seems to start the moment she arrives."
"I'm so sorry, Arnold."
"Thanks. It's for the best, really. We've not been happy for a while. I'm mostly worried about my four-year-old son. We've already decided that he'll be staying with me and I'm just not sure I can afford to manage on my salary alone."
"This has got to be very hard on you."
Arnold nods in agreement.
"What are you planning to do for child care?"
"I'm pretty lucky on that front. My mother looks

after Kirk during the morning. He's in preschool in the afternoon and she takes him there and picks him up afterwards."

"That's excellent." Martha pauses before subtly shifting topics. "Now what can I do to help you regain your focus, so you can earn the promotion necessary to give you a little more cash flow?"

"Martha, you've done a lot today just by listening. I think the rest is mostly up to me."

"You feel that you're getting clear direction and support?"

"And adequate and appropriate training too, which is helping me gain recognition and proper rewards."

The group laughed loudly. It was clear that they had absorbed the CARE concept training that Charlie had given them earlier in the week.

Charlie couldn't help but join them. "Very good, guys. Very good," he chuckled. "So, I take it you're done?"

Will looked at Molly. "I think so."

"I'm pretty comfortable with the role play. I certainly learned a lot," Molly said.

"Molly, you taught me a lot. This experience was really enlightening. Thank you, and thank you, Charlie," Will said sincerely.

"You're welcome, Will. But tell me, do you feel that this exercise resulted in a two-way empathetic path being established?"

Will thought for a moment before replying, "Well, not really. I mean, Martha knows a lot about the pressures Arnold's under, but Arnold really didn't gain much insight into what she's up against."

"I agree," Charlie said. He addressed the room again. "Remember, the foundation of CARE is empathy and it is always a two-way street." He looked at Will and Molly. "Do you guys want to take a stab at expanding your new-found empathetic relationship?"

Molly smiled. "Why not? Besides, I kind of like this 'being the boss' thing."

"And I'm enjoying reporting to you," Will added with a smile. "How about if I start?"

"Thanks, Martha, you've been a big help. I'll pull up my socks and start delivering what I'm capable of."

"That will help me. Thanks."

"Martha, what else can I do to ease your situation? I think I know you pretty well and I get the sense there are some behind-the-scenes pressures that you are protecting us from."

Martha manages a small smile. "You're very perceptive, Arnold. The productivity levels for our unit have dropped dramatically this past quarter, and I need to turn things around quickly or —"

Arnold rescued his boss. "Say no more. I've got some productivity improvement ideas that I've been dying to share with somebody and I know that . . ." — Will looked at Oscar — ". . . Orville here has a few ideas as well. Why don't we spend an hour at the end of the day to see what we can up with as a team?"

"Really?"

"Really."

"Beautiful, just beautiful," said Charlie, applauding. "What happened here, gang?"

Oscar — "Orville" — responded, "Other than giving me a new name, which I hate, by the way, these guys formed a really strong two-way empathetic bond."

"And on a level that was way beyond the context of this role play," Will added. "Charlie, I'm impressed by what you've done for me personally today, and for what I believe you've given all of us by exposing us to CARE. Thank you."

"My pleasure."

7

Clear
Direction

Chelsea Vail sensed a presence in the doorway of her office and looked up to see her grandfather. He was dressed in a beautifully tailored navy suit and looked very distinguished.

"You're back!"

"Flew in last night from L.A. right after the last session with Will Riley's team."

"You must be tired?"

"Not too bad. I managed to catch a few winks on the flight, which helped."

"Well, you certainly don't look tired. In fact, I'd go so far as to say you are looking very dapper, indeed. Nice rags!" Chelsea exclaimed.

Charlie smiled, "Hey, I've got to look the part, right? Have you got a minute to chat?"

"Sure, but it'll cost you a hug."

"That's the main reason I'm here."

They embraced warmly and then sat down at the meeting table in the corner of Chelsea's office.

"So, how did it go in L.A.?"

"Pretty well, I think. I've completed the role-play

sessions with the Western Division team, and I think there was a pretty big breakthrough."

"You tackled the tough one first."

"I hope you're right. Will didn't really need much help in the first three parts of CARE. We were able to develop a few good action plans, but for the most part Will's pretty strong, from a management fundamentals point of view. What he really needed was to build a solid foundation for those fundamental skills."

"Empathy."

"Right. Over the course of the week we went through some pretty tough role plays, and I think the message got through."

"That's great. I have a lot of respect for Will's abilities. If you've 'humanized' him through CARE, he's going to be a tremendous asset to this organization."

"I think so, too."

"So what now?"

"Next stop is Stan Cox's division. Can you give me any insight into what I can expect?"

"Stan's a really nice guy. I'm told that his people really like him. He's a little scattered, though, and I understand he can't be counted on when his people really need him."

Charlie smiled. "Gee, could you be more specific?"

Chelsea laughed. "Okay, this guy needs help with the C in CARE, in a big way."

"I gathered that." Charlie rose and again embraced his granddaughter. "Thanks, I'll let you know how it turns out."

ZIMCO CENTRAL DIVISION, CHICAGO

It took Charlie all of ten minutes to decide that he liked Stan Cox. The man had an extremely warm personality. He laughed readily and often, and used his wonderful sense of humor frequently and appropriately. Charlie also decided that Chelsea's assessment of Stan Cox was accurate. He was definitely in need of CARE, and the focus of the role-play sessions that Charlie would conduct with him would emphasize the importance of clear direction and support.

Stan Cox's team had assembled in the boardroom, and Charlie was enjoying the way they related to each other. They clearly took pleasure in one another's company and were very comfortable with their boss's relaxed style. They had already been through one role play to reinforce empathy as the foundation of CARE. Now it was time to address the primary weakness in their part of the Zimco organization.

Charlie looked at Stan. "Well, boss, are you ready to do a little acting?"

"You must be looking for a leading-man type."

"Exactly," Charlie chuckled. He flipped open his CARE bible. "How about you playing the role of Warren?" He handed Stan a role-play sheet. "And Burt, how about you playing the role of Lester?"

"Nice name. Don't you have any macho names in

there, maybe Lance or Dirk?"

"Sorry, you're a Lester this time around." Charlie passed copies of the role-play documents to everyone in the room. "Let's take a few minutes to read through these and then we'll get started."

Role Play #2
Stan in the role of "Warren"

You have been employed by your company for over fifteen years and have spent the last seven years in a senior management capacity. You have always been well respected by your staff and by upper management, but lately it appears that your star is beginning to dim. Your department had poor results last year and you are not off to a great start this year. Still, you're confident that things will turn around.

You have a new boss, Lester, for whom you are quickly losing respect. Lester is a really nice person and very likeable, but he is providing no direction about what he expects from you or from your division. Also, since Lester has been in place, your access to the corporate strategic plan has been cut off. Yours is an industry that is rapidly changing, and access to information on a timely basis is critical.

The company's new president is conducting business plan reviews with each division manager. Yours is scheduled for a week from today. It's critical that your plan reflect the current corporate strategies. That would not be a problem if you knew what they were. You decide to meet with Lester to help you prepare for your plan review. He is alone in his office when you knock on his door and enter . . .

Burt in the role of "Lester"

You've recently transferred to a new position in the company and have responsibility for the national sales organization. You consider this the perfect job. You've always had a way with people, and customers love you. Your sense of humor is much appreciated and your laissez-faire attitude has always created a very relaxed work environment. Your new position affords you access to the real power base of the company, and you have already been given copies of the company's new strategic plan, which will reshape the organization's direction in the coming years.

You're not a detail guy, however — never have been — and although you have had the plan for almost a month, you haven't got around to reading it yet. You've heard it discussed at so many meetings, however, that you have picked up enough understanding of the new direction to get by. Besides, you are primarily a sales guy and what you need to do is drive sales. Your philosophy could be summed up as, "Leave strategy to the academics and leave the real work to the salespeople."

One of your sales directors, Warren, has asked to see you to discuss his upcoming business plan review. You don't know Warren very well yet, but you do know that his results were poor last year, and he and his team are off to a weak start this year. You're already wondering whether he's the right guy for the job. There is a knock on the door and Warren enters your office . . .

"Everybody ready?" Charlie asked.

"I've got to play golf in half an hour. Can I just fire this guy and get on with my game?" Burt said.

Charlie waited for the laughter to subside and then replied, "Hey, Burt, whatever you want. There are no rules in the role plays."

"Great."

"Just remember," Stan added, "who the real boss is when the role play ends."

Burt looked at one of his peers. "Cancel my golf game. In fact, cancel my membership. I need to spend time with my best employee, Warren."

More laughter ensued. "Good one, Burt," Charlie said. "Now, please, let's get to work. Take it from the knock."

Lester looks up to see Warren entering his office. "Warren, c'mon in. How's it going?"

"Things are looking up. We're close to landing the Willow deal."

"What's that one about?"

"Remember the Egyptian guys who are building that new facility near Meadowvale?"

"Oh, yeah, I think you sent me a note on that one."

"Right. Anyway, I think we're going to close it, which will get us back on track for the quarter."

"Good. So, what did you want to see me about?"

"As you know, next week I'm presenting my business plan to our new president. I think it's important that I deliver a quality plan and I'm feeling a little ill-equipped to pull together a comprehensive document."

"You have Krista Bradley on your team. She's worked with me before on presentations, and she's really good at this stuff. Why don't you hand it off to her?"

"Krista is helping, Lester, but my problem isn't with the presentation's structure. It's with the content. I need to have a better understanding of our corporate direction in order to ensure that my sales strategies reflect that direction."

"Is that all? That's not a problem." Lester pauses for a minute. "At last week's senior managers' conference, we talked about the need to have more of our commodity products sold through an e-channel we're planning to develop —"

"An e-channel?"

"Yeah, Internet stuff — electronic ordering and the like."

"Okay."

"And we're going to try and move up the value chain in terms of the products and services we carry. More consulting services and less commodity — stuff like that."

"How do we intend to do this?"

"That's your job, buddy — to figure that stuff out."

Charlie interrupted, "Okay, let's pause right there. Comments or observations, anybody?"

Brian Andrews piped up, "It's pretty clear that these

guys are not connecting. They're operating on really different planes."

"I think that's a pretty fair comment." Charlie turned toward the role-play participants. "Warren, do you feel you're getting the information you need from Lester?"

"Not even close. He's giving me what seems to be an anecdotal view, from 50,000 feet. There's nothing here that I'd feel comfortable about incorporating into my business plan presentation."

"Anybody have any suggestions?" Charlie asked.

Sally Hanlon spoke. "Well, Lester's clearly not a detail guy, and it appears that Warren is. So Warren should probably try and take on the role of detail guy on Lester's team. This would deliver good value to his boss by filling a gap in Lester's skill set, and it would provide Warren with the information he needs to do his job."

"This is great," Charlie responded. "What Sally's suggesting is that Warren and Lester work toward forming a new relationship, one that has a stronger, more empathetic foundation, and that will yield benefits for the company as well. Sally, any ideas as to how they might do this?"

Before she could reply, Stan said, "How about if I give it a try?"

"Great," said Charlie.

"Lester, at the senior managers' conference, did you receive any information on the corporation's strategic direction?"

"Our CEO, Lyle, gave us his perspective on where he

believes we need to head in the next few years."

"Great, did you get a copy of his presentation?"

"The slides he used are in the book they gave us at the conference." Lester points to his credenza. "It's right there. I don't know how valuable the presentation slides are without hearing the words around them, but you're welcome to look at them."

"Thanks. I'll talk to Lyle's assistant and see who pulled the presentation together. Whoever did is likely pretty current with Lyle's strategy, including his background material. If you like, I'd be happy to present the strategy at our next unit meeting."

"That would be great."

"Happy to do it."

Charlie interrupted the role play, "Okay, that was excellent, guys. Anybody have any comments on what just happened here?"

Sally raised her hand.

"Sally?"

"I think Warren just applied the empathy part of CARE in a very big way."

"Can you elaborate?"

"As I said earlier, Lester is not the least bit detail oriented. He's a sales leader and he's not into the whole future direction shtick. He's a meet-your-quota kind of manager, and appears to be a great guy to work with. Warren, however, is more strategically focused, and isn't comfortable in his job unless he feels plugged into the big picture. He isn't getting the information he needs from his boss, so, instead of living with the situation, which is very stressful and limiting for him, he fixed the problem by *becoming* the boss for this particular project. His empathy for Lester allowed him to realize his goal and to help his boss and his teammates at the same time. The whole team will benefit by getting the clear direction that has been lacking since Lester took over."

"Exactly," Charlie confirmed. To the group he said, "You've now witnessed an excellent example of the *clear direction* component of CARE, leveraged by the power of empathy."

The participants nodded in unison. Nobody offered a comment, so Charlie continued, "What we now need to do as a team is to define our goals relative to clear direction, identify any roadblocks that might prevent us from achieving our goals, and define the action plans necessary to realize these goals."

Charlie moved to his laptop and tapped on the keyboard. An image appeared on the screen behind him. "Here's a template that I've used many times, and that I've found very effective in completing this exercise."

**CARE: GOAL IDENTIFICATION AND
ACTION PLAN DEVELOPMENT**

What we need: Our Goals

1.

2.

3.

CARE: GOAL IDENTIFICATION AND
ACTION PLAN DEVELOPMENT cont'd

What addressing these needs will accomplish:
Strategic Intent
1.
2.
3.
Roadblocks or obstacles to achieving our goals
1.
2.
3.
How we will deliver on our goals: Our Action Plans
1.
2.
3.
Who is accountable for delivery of our action plans
1.
2.
3.
Our measures of success: Deliverables
1.
2.
3.

"Is this done on an individual or a departmental level?" Stan asked.

"It starts at the top, Stan, with you, and it trickles down through the organization. So the answer to your question is that it's done at both the individual and the departmental level, if one accepts that your individual CARE contract represents the departmental direction."

"That makes sense," Stan replied. "Shall I take a shot at completing this template?"

"Let's do it," Charlie replied.

The goal definition and action plan development exercise took less than an hour to complete. It was apparent to all the workshop participants that Stan had an excellent understanding of the goals for his division and knew what actions needed to be taken in order to deliver on them. Now, thanks to CARE, the rest of his core team also had a clear understanding of the direction for their division.

Burt Thatcher captured the mood of Stan's team accurately. "Stan, this is so helpful. Seeing your personal CARE contract has really helped me understand what's required of me in my job to help you and the organization succeed."

Stan smiled. "I feel better too, Burt. And I can't wait to have CARE contracts completed for our entire organization."

Clear
Support

Charlie observed with satisfaction the healthy interaction among the Central Division team members as they prepared to re-engage in the CARE learning process. He had seen this so many times before. The positive outcome of yesterday's session had created an energy level and an air of excitement that promised to make today's session even more fruitful.

"Okay, who wants to role-play today?" Charlie asked. Everyone raised a hand except Burt and Stan — they'd had their turn. Charlie knew this was a common occurrence with CARE. Once exposed to the power of the role plays, everyone wanted to be part of them.

"Everybody's keen. Terrific! How about Sally and Brian having a go at it?"

Role Play #3
Sally in the role of "Jessica"

You are an executive who handles major accounts, and you are currently working on a large proposal for your most important account. The situation is very competitive, but you've managed to get to the final stage in the decision-making process. You've been told that the deal is yours to lose. The one hurdle you have to overcome to win the business, however, is a major one. You have to guarantee delivery of the solution you've proposed within six weeks of contract signature. The contracts will be signed in two weeks' time, which gives your company eight weeks to deliver, with substantial penalties for non-delivery.

Your solutions support team is telling you they can't possibly commit to the delivery date you need to close this deal. You have communicated your requirements to the vice-president responsible for solutions support, but to no avail. You were simply told, "I don't have the resources to make this happen in the time frames you need. The only way I can possibly agree to what you want is if our president is willing to delay another customer's implementation — or if she's willing to cough up the money to bring in some subcontractors to work this project. Otherwise, it just isn't going to happen."

Your company's president, Olivia, is very autocratic and not approachable. Your only chance to get your deal through is to convince your boss, Ted, to talk to Olivia. That is a problem. Ted is a pleasant enough guy, but he's the kind of person who will agree to do whatever is asked of him, and then never do a thing. You desperately need the commission from this sale. Somehow you have to persuade your boss to convince Olivia to commit to meeting the customer's demands. You approach Ted, who is sitting quietly in his office, reading a book . . .

Brian in the role of "Ted"

You are highly regarded as a resource within the company, but, in your view, you are totally out of your element leading the sales group. Your formal education and career interests lie in the area of strategic planning, and your personal career plan has you slated to move into that job at the end of this calendar year, when the company's VP of corporate strategy retires. You can hardly wait. You were put into the sales job to groom you for bigger things, but after two years you've had enough grooming. Sales and the day-to-day problems that are part of the sales process are definitely not your thing.

To complicate matters, your new boss, Olivia, is very focused on sales and reluctant to engage in conversation about corporate strategy. Also, because you've brought her several issues requiring resolution since she's been in the job, she has recently questioned your level of autonomy and your valued "high resource" stature. You're determined to stay out of her way until you can make your move into the VP role you covet. And, as she's made so clear, she doesn't want to be distracted from her work by day-to-day problems. You look up as Jessica, one of your stronger account executives, enters your office . . .

It appeared to Charlie that everyone had finished reading the role-play staging documents. "You guys ready?"

"Ready and willing," said Sally, "and 'Ted,' I'm warning you, 'Jessica' ain't happy!"

Her role-play partner laughed. "Then let's see what I can do to make you even more miserable."

"Hi, Ted. Do you have a moment?"

"Jessica, oh . . . come on in." Ted puts down his book. "Catching up on my reading," he says, almost apologetically. "*Ten Trends That Will Shape the New Millennium.* Have you read it?"

"No, haven't seen that one."

"It's excellent. You should give it a read when you get the chance."

"Yeah."

Ted gestures her to sit at the worktable in his office. She does so and he joins her. "What's up?"

"I need your help. I've closed the Rand deal, subject to being able to deliver our solution within six weeks of signing the contract. It's worth close to $24 million over the next four years."

"Congratulations! That's outstanding."

"Maybe . . . The key to our getting the business is delivering within the six-week time frame. If we can't commit to this by the end of the day, and don't agree to stiff penalties for non-delivery, we'll lose the business. Our major competitor has already stepped up to this, I'm told. But Rand wants to partner with us — it's ours to lose."

"Then let's just do it."

"I wish it were that simple," replies Jessica. "Tyler is saying 'no can do.' His team is tapped out and the only way he'll agree to this is if Olivia agrees to either delay another customer's implementation, or approve his hiring outside contractors — which his budget doesn't allow for."

"Do we know if any of our customers might be willing to delay their implementations?"

"I've checked it out with my peers. It's not going to happen."

"Is there any chance Rand can delay their implementation?"

"I've exhausted that possibility. There's no chance. Their requirement stems from the recent spin-off of one of their smaller divisions. They're legally obligated to have the new system in place and operational within six weeks."

Ted runs his hands over his face. "Maybe I'll talk to Stephen, our VP in solutions support."

"You can try, but he'll tell you his hands are tied. You're going to need to involve Olivia. I talked to her assistant before coming to see you. She's in this morning and she has a couple of open slots on her calendar."

"Uh . . . sure, I'll give her a call and see what we can do."

Charlie interrupted, "Okay, let's stop here for a moment. Jessica, are you confident that Ted is going to do what needs to be done to close your deal?"

"Absolutely not. I have the feeling he's not going to do a thing and my deal and my commission will go down the drain."

"Do you have any idea why he seems reluctant to do what needs to be done?"

Sally paused. "That's a good question. He's certainly

not handling things the way I would. If I were —"

Charlie interrupted, "Sorry, Jessica, stop right there for a moment." He turned to face Brian. "Ted, how are you feeling right now?"

"Pressured. There are very good reasons why I can't take this problem to Olivia for resolution. If I —"

"Ted, sorry for interrupting," Charlie said, "but let me make an observation. This role play is set up to illustrate the lack of a clear support contract between you two, and that fact is very apparent. But you won't ever establish such a contract unless you develop a relationship foundation based on empathy. It's apparent that each of you is working to a personal agenda. You need to get past that and try to live in each other's shoes a little bit."

The two actors nodded in agreement.

"Any ideas as to how we might accomplish this, Charlie?" Brian asked.

"I think you're closer to understanding Jessica's situation than she is to understanding yours. Maybe the key is for Jessica to try and see things a little more from your perspective."

"I have an idea," Sally said. "Let me give it a whirl."

"Ted, can I make a suggestion?"

"By all means."

"I sense that you're reluctant to bring this problem to Olivia, and I'm guessing it's because she's got a million things on her plate and you'd rather not bring her another one."

"Something like that . . ."

"Okay, so let's not bring her the problem. Let's bring her the solution."

"Which is . . . ?" Ted asks.

"The Rand deal is so big that it almost guarantees we'll exceed our year-end target. One more like it, which I'm sure we can land, and we'll be well over plan for the year. This kind of achievement should allow us to overspend our budget, shouldn't it?"

"Not necessarily, but it would certainly allow us to defend an overspend."

"Great. Let's tell Tyler that we'll pay for whatever outside help he needs to deliver this solution. If it means we're overspending our budget, we'll live with the consequences — which shouldn't be great, given our overachievement of our revenue targets. We'll let Olivia know that we're doing this, of course. If she's got a problem with it, she'll have until late this afternoon to speak up. If she doesn't, then we'll just go ahead and do it. What do you think?"

"Great idea."

"That was great, guys," said Charlie. "Do you think you'll hear from Olivia?"

"I think she'll be thrilled at winning such a big deal and very pleased to know she didn't have to get involved in solving yet another of Ted's problems," Brian offered.

"What did you learn, Sally?" Charlie asked.

"I guess I learned that I have a role to play in getting

the support I need to do my job. I can't just dump my problems on my boss and expect him to solve them. There are likely to be dynamics in play that I don't understand, which could jeopardize my end goal. I certainly need to keep asking for support when I need it, but I should always try and bring a potential solution along with the problem."

"How about you, Brian?"

"It reinforced in my mind the importance of supporting your people when they need you, while reinforcing that it's okay — even desirable — to get your people involved in helping define, and even helping you get, the support they need."

"Excellent. Does anybody else have observations to make?"

Stan Cox raised his hand. "I have to confess that the last two role plays hit pretty close to home. I'm guessing they were selected to show me that I need to provide clearer direction to the members of my division and to give them better support."

"Stan," Charlie said, "I did select the role plays very carefully, and I did try and address what I perceive to be a weakness in your division. But it's important for you, and for the other people in this room, to know that this is not just about making you a better division leader. It's about making each of you, and ultimately all the members of your division, better employees and thus more effective as an entity. Clear direction and support contracts, built on a foundation of empathy, will help you accomplish that goal."

Adequate
Training

Matt McMaster looked up to see Charlie standing in the doorway of his office. He motioned the older man to enter and quickly wrapped up his phone call. "That was Stan Cox. He tells me you did a wonderful job in the week you spent with his division."

"That's nice feedback. Thanks. They were a good team to work with. Stan's a good man and he has the makings of an excellent CARE manager."

"I think he does now. He explained to me how you used the role plays to reinforce the importance of clear direction and support."

"We covered a few areas, but we concentrated our efforts on the C of CARE. I think the division will be stronger for it."

"I'm convinced they will be. Look at this — it's what Stan and I were just discussing."

Charlie reached across the desk and took the document from Matt.

---

*CARE Support Contract between Stan Cox
and Matt McMaster*

Matt's commitments
- I will return your phone calls and e-mails promptly.
- I will not micromanage your job.
- I will allow you to make your own decisions.
- I will be available to you as a sounding board to assist you in making better decisions.
- I will act promptly on issues you bring to me that require resolution (i.e., no procrastination).
- I will ensure that you are kept current on the corporation's strategic direction.
- I will represent you and your initiatives fairly within the company.

Stan's commitments
- I will return your calls and e-mails promptly.
- I will publicly and internally support you and your stated direction.
- I will assist you in the performance of your duties when asked to do so.
- I will involve you in my job only when I need your experience, influence, or support to make me more successful in mine.
- I will keep you well informed on issues within my division that might affect you and/or the company positively or negatively.

Charlie quickly scanned the CARE contract. "It looks as if Stan took the CARE training to heart. This is excellent. Do you see the value in this as well?"

"I'm learning that I'm a bit of a procrastinator and that when one of my managers brings me something that requires my involvement or approval, I need to make quicker decisions."

"You're slowing down the business process . . .?"

"I didn't think I'd been here long enough to do that yet, but yes, I'm getting a bit of a reputation for being slow to respond to my people. So this CARE contract is very helpful to me. The last thing I want to be perceived as is a blocker."

"Good."

"Stan's also in the process of creating CARE direction and support contracts for every member of his division."

"That will take a little longer to implement."

"Absolutely, but he's determined to have all the CARE contracts in place within the next two months."

"That's marvelous."

"So is CARE, Charlie, and you've clearly done a wonderful job in driving home its value."

"Thank you."

"What's next?"

"I'm slated to spend the next week in Toronto with Donna Maples's Northern Division team."

"Any first impressions?"

"Well, I spent a couple of days poking around in preparation for my CARE training. There are a number of problems I think we can address."

"Anything in particular jump out at you?"

"Well, there's not a whole lot of training going on and the money that is being spent on training doesn't appear to be going to the right places."

ZIMCO NORTHERN DIVISION, TORONTO

The team that Charlie assembled for the first role-play session in Donna Maples's division was selected from throughout the organization and represented various levels within the business. They all had two things in common: they were relatively new in their current positions, and none of them had been properly trained for the tasks they were expected to perform.

Charlie opened his role-play bible to the section he'd selected earlier. "Donna? Are you ready to take on the role of Marion?"

"Sure."

"Good. Betty, how about you taking on the role of Marion's boss, Doris?"

"Ooh . . . I get to be my boss's boss. This should be fun." She smiled mischievously. "Can I fire her if she steps out of line?"

The members of the team laughed.

"I'll leave that decision to you," Charlie replied. "Just remember where you'll be tomorrow morning."

"Maybe I'll give her a big raise instead."

"That might be wise," Donna said.

Role Play #4

Donna in the role of "Marion"

You are a single mother of two who is struggling to make ends meet. You have been employed at a local high-technology firm for close to two years, and have recently been promoted to the bid-response center as a documentation specialist. This is a salaried position that will allow you to earn an additional $5,000 annually. Finally you are in a position to support your family properly. There may even be a little money left over to take an occasional vacation.

Your first month on the job went smoothly, but a new documentation system has just been installed and you are having trouble adjusting to the software. It's essentially the same as the previous version, but there are enough subtle differences in the program to slow down your production. Since the bid-support process is akin to an assembly line, your reduced output is slowing down the entire team. You've had to work longer hours and so has the team — all because you have become a bottleneck in the bid-response process. Your supervisor, Doris, is aware of the problem and who is causing it. She is not happy, and you are worried that you might be fired before you can learn the intricacies of the new software and return to your former level of production. You are consulting the instruction manual, trying to figure out how to use the desktop publishing software to insert a photo in the bid, when Doris approaches. She is clearly angry . . .

Betty in the role of "Doris"

You are a new supervisor, still in your probation period. Your review is due within the month and things have been going well until just recently. Your best documentation specialist has gone on maternity leave, and her replacement, Marion, is a disaster. Her job demands that she be fully conversant with the various software packages used in bid responses, but she is constantly checking the instruction manuals. Because her role is pivotal in the bid-response process, the bids that she is working on are being tremendously delayed. Just last week, one of those bids was late and was refused by the customer, until your company's president called the customer's senior officer and convinced him to accept the bid. You have been told in no uncertain terms that if this happens again you can kiss your supervisory job goodbye. You've worked long and hard to get this job, and you're not going to blow your big opportunity because of one incompetent employee. Just moments ago, one of the sales account representatives complained that the bid Marion is currently working on is late and he is worried that it will not get to the customer on schedule. The time has come for you to have it out with Marion. You approach and find her with her nose in a manual . . .

Charlie scanned the room. It appeared that everybody had finished reading the role-play sheets. "Okay, shall we get started?"

"Marion, have I not told you that I don't want you reading

instruction manuals on the job? You're supposed to know how to use this software. That's why you are in the job."

"Sorry, Doris. I know the basics, but this version is different from what I'm used to. It has a lot more features and I need to use the manual to complete the work as professionally as possible."

Charlie interrupted, "Let's stop there for a moment. Comments, anybody?"

One of Donna's managers, Jim O'Reilly, raised his hand.

"Jim?"

"Praise in public, reprimand in private."

Charlie looked at Betty. "Jim makes a good point. Though it's possible that you were assuming your role play was taking place in a private setting . . ."

Betty sheepishly replied, "I'm afraid not. I guess this shows that I'm not a manager, huh?"

"Not at all. It means that you are learning how to become a CARE manager. How about if we pick up where we left off, and let's assume you've taken Marion aside, as Jim is suggesting."

"Gotcha."

"Marion, as I've told you before, I can't afford to have you training yourself on the job. You are slowing down the whole process. I want you to learn the new system quickly, and to do it on your own time. Do I make myself clear?"

"Yes, I —"

"Sorry, Charlie, I have to step out of the role play for a moment. This whole thing is hitting way too close to home."

"In what way, Donna?" Charlie asked.

"This is embarrassing to admit, but I seem to recall saying the same thing to Betty that Doris just said to Marion."

"And how do you feel about that now?"

"Not very good. In the role play I don't have the time or money to train myself outside business hours, and I'm resenting Doris's attitude. I'm finding myself wondering if Betty might be feeling the same way about me. I really don't know much about *her* personal circumstances. I've just assumed —"

Charlie interrupted, "Donna, you're having a real CARE breakthrough moment here, which is great. What you're relating to is the importance of empathizing with your people. And you can't empathize with them unless you understand what's going on in their lives."

"I'm beginning to understand that."

Charlie addressed Betty, "Why don't you slip back into the role play to see if you can deal with this situation?" He looked at Donna. "Is that okay with you?"

"Sure."

"Good. Marion, Doris — over to you."

"Marion, what do you think you need to learn in order to deliver the kind of work volume and quality that earned you this job?"

"I need to have proper training on the new software. I

think I could learn everything I need to know with two full days of training."

"And then you'd be fully productive?"

"Absolutely."

"Can you not complete this training on your own time? I know there are courses available on evenings and weekends."

"Doris, I'm a single mom. I have two young children and no family support system in this city. I race out of here every night to pick up my kids at the sitter before six. My evenings and weekends are a blur. I just don't have time to take training courses on my own time. Maybe someday my situation will improve, but today all I can give is the ten hours a day I spend in this office. I hope you understand . . ."

"I do. Thanks for explaining what you're dealing with. Let's book you for a couple of training days as soon as this job is finished."

"That would be great."

"We do, however, still have to meet the deadline for this particular bid response. And believe me, my boss and the organization won't tolerate our missing another deadline. Are you aware of what happened on the last one we missed?"

"I heard that our president had to call in some favors to get our late bid accepted."

"Exactly. And that situation has raised doubts about our team's ability to deliver."

"I'm so sorry, Doris, I didn't know that things were so serious . . ."

"We'll get past it, I'm sure. And once you are properly trained, I'm confident we won't have to deal with any missed commitments in the future. In the meantime, how certain are you that we can meet the deadline we're facing right now?"

Marion scans her desk. "I still have quite a bit to do. It's the graphs that I'm struggling with. Once I get past those, I'll be able to fly through the rest of the document."

"Okay, here's what we're going to do: I'll do the graphs and you concentrate on the text." Doris looks at her watch. "We'll touch base in two hours to see how far we've got."

"Okay, that was terrific," Charlie said. "Donna, how do you feel?"

"Thankful, on a couple of levels: my boss, Marion, bailed me out of a jam by empathizing with my situation and, more important, I learned that I have to put a little energy into creating empathetic relationships with my people — starting with Betty."

"Betty? Any comments or observations?"

"Much the same. I learned something about the pressures my boss is under and that I, too, need to empathize with her situation more than I have in the past. Thanks for the lesson in CARE. It was a good learning experience, and I'm confident it will help both of us do better in our jobs."

10

Appropriate
Training

Charlie looked at the list of names on the paper in front of him as the participants settled into their chairs for the day's CARE session. "Everybody well rested after yesterday's session?"

Charlie's question was greeted with nods and a chorus of affirmatives.

"Good. Now, let's see. I think the only members of the team who haven't participated in a role-play session are Wayne and Sherry. Are you two up to the challenge?"

"As long as I get to be the boss," Sherry said with a grin.

Wayne looked at her and smiled. "I can handle that."

"Good," said Charlie. He reached into his binder and pulled out the role-play sheets. "Wayne, you are playing the role of Clarence, and, Sherry, you are Isabelle."

Role Play #5
Wayne in the role of "Clarence"

You are a sales representative at a very progressive high-technology company that invests heavily in training its people. Yours is an industry that is changing very rapidly and it is absolutely critical that you stay on top of current trends.

One of the things you like most about your job is that you are provided with a personal training budget that you control. You are expected to use this budget for your own self-development.

Your boss, Isabelle, is a really nice, caring manager with whom you enjoy working. She is also very hands-off in her managerial style, a trait you like. Isabelle's philosophy is pretty simple: "Bring in the numbers and I will leave you alone." This has never presented a problem before, but lately you've had trouble meeting your sales quota. You know what the problem is: you are just not current with some of the new technology, and this prevents you from presenting your solutions to customers in a credible manner. You know you need additional training on emerging technologies but, unfortunately, you exhausted your personal training budget when you attended an industry conference in Hawaii last spring. Your year-end is six months away. If you don't receive some in-depth training on the new technology within the next couple of weeks, you are certain to miss your sales targets — and may even lose your job. Lately you have been picking the brains of a couple of your engineer team members for answers. This is helping somewhat, but it's not giving you the insight you need. You also sense that your engineering colleagues are becoming a little annoyed, particularly as they exhausted their training budgets on an in-town course on the new technology. Several of the other sales representatives were with you at the conference in Hawaii, and they too are struggling with the new technology — and leaning on the same two engineers for help.

The latest sales reports are out and you have had another poor month. Isabelle calls and says she wants to see you immediately . . .

Sherry in the role of "Isabelle"

You have been the regional sales manager for almost six years. You have always enjoyed success on the job, but your results to date in this calendar year are behind forecast. Your boss, a very autocratic, detail-oriented manager, is starting to ask some tough questions. You're worried that if you don't turn the results around, it could cost you your job. You've also received a number of customer complaints lately, some of which have been routed to the company's president. The theme of the complaints is consistent: "Your people don't know what they're talking about."

One of your usually reliable representatives, Clarence, has been the target of several of the complaints. Your boss wants to send a message to the force to shape up and he is hinting strongly that you should upgrade your sales team by firing the weaker players. Clarence is clearly in his sights, and the latest sales report hasn't weakened your boss's resolve. You have to talk to Clarence about his poor performance and what he needs to do about it. You invite him to see you in your office . . .

"Hey, Izzie, how's it going?"

"Have a seat, please, Clarence."

The sales representative sits down in front of his boss's desk. "You wanted to see me?"

"Clarence, I need to know what's happening with your results. You've been a solid rep up till now, but your results are terrible this year. I need to know what you plan on doing about it."

"Izz, I know my results are poor so far, but I'm confident I can still make my year-end target."

"Based on what? I accessed your pending sales funnel this morning, and it's almost empty. I don't think there's any way you can deliver your numbers this year."

"There are a couple of deals that aren't in the funnel."

"A couple of deals won't make a difference, based on what I saw. And I don't see one proposal for our new IP World product. This solution should be flying off the shelf and you've not made a single sale."

"I . . . Isabelle, I don't really understand the IP World product."

"Is that the problem? Then get whatever training you need. You've got a personal training budget — use it!"

Clarence avoids his boss's gaze.

"Clarence?"

"I . . . I exhausted my training budget in first quarter."

"You're allocated $12,000 for personal training. How could you possibly have exhausted the entire amount in first quarter?"

"I went to a conference in Hawaii."

"I'm aware of that, but $12,000 for a conference? You're not serious!"

"There was a week-long seminar on electronic commerce that I thought looked interesting."

"Clarence, you don't even sell electronic commerce. What kind of boondoggle were you on?"

"I . . . I wasn't thinking. I thought I had enough of a foundation in Internet protocol to pick up the intricacies of the IP World product, but it's way more technical than I thought it would be, and I'm lost. My customers' technical people know more about IP than I do."

"Clarence, I'm afraid I'm going to have to —"

Charlie jumped in, "Okay, before you fire young Clarence here, which I think is where you are heading —."

"Aw, I was dying to fire the slacker!" Sherry said with a laugh.

"And you'll pay for that when the games are over," Wayne said, smiling.

Charlie took control. "Okay, does anybody have any ideas as to what Sherry's next step should be?"

Donna Maples responded, "I think a little empathy is in order."

"Can you elaborate for us, Donna?"

"Sure, Charlie. This is not a situation where Clarence is not capable of selling, which would suggest that dismissal is the appropriate action. He has been a successful salesperson for a number of years.

"Isabelle is dealing with a case of inappropriate training. Clarence was allowed to determine his own training program, and he used terrible judgment in using his training dollars on what was for him a rather meaningless conference. Isabelle now needs to put herself in Clarence's shoes and then find a way to re-establish him as a strong contributor, by finding a win-win way to get him the training he needs."

Charlie looked to the role-players. "Donna has a good suggestion. Sherry, would you like to try it on for size?"

"I think I know where she's heading. Sure."

"Good, let's do it."

"Clarence, you are a very good sales representative and you've delivered strong results every year that you've been in the company. I'm confident that, with the proper training, you can continue to make a strong contribution to this organization."

"Thank you, Isabelle, I appreciate the kind words."

"The problem we now face is this: you've spent your personal training budget, and you desperately need specific training. How do you suggest we address this?"

Clarence hesitates before answering, "I'm not sure. Maybe I have to consider paying for some of the training myself."

"That thought has certainly crossed my mind. I have another suggestion, though."

Clarence looks at his boss expectantly. "Yeah . . . ?"

"I'll fund the training you require, but I'll recover its cost from the commissions you will earn when you achieve 100 percent of your annual plan. If I recall correctly, when you hit plan, you achieve an immediate $12,000 bonus. Is that right?"

"That's right. So, I can keep the commissions I

earn before I hit plan, and I keep any overachievement dollars . . ."

"Right. The only thing you forfeit is the bonus you get for hitting plan."

"What if I don't reach 100 percent of my sales target?"

"Then we both lose. I've lost the money I've invested in you, and you've lost my respect . . . and maybe you'll lose your job."

Clarence looks at his boss with admiration. "Isabelle, you're being more than fair. In some companies, I would have been fired on the spot. I won't let you down."

"That possibility is the furthest thing from my mind."

"And . . . break!" Charlie said. "That was excellent — a fine demonstration of a win-win solution, founded on empathy. Well done!"

"Same goes for you, Charlie," Donna Maples stated. "I can't speak for the members of my team, but I'm guessing that they feel the same way I do. You and CARE have taught me a lot."

Recognition

"Charlie, c'mon in. I hope you don't mind, but I was already scheduled to meet with Chelsea when you called for an appointment, and I didn't think you'd mind if she sat in on our discussion."

"Well, I guess that'll be all right, Matt." Charlie moved to his granddaughter and embraced her warmly. "You never call, you never write . . ."

"I called you twice last week, and you still haven't called me back."

"The boss has me working too hard to return personal calls."

Matt and Chelsea both laughed. "I'm pleased to hear that, Charlie," Matt said. "I love knowing that people are working too hard to have time for a personal life. How's your golf game?"

"I don't think you're going to have as tough a time beating me in a rematch, which I'm sure is part of your overall plan."

"Exactly."

Charlie changed topic to the issue at hand. "The CARE training is going pretty well, I think. I've just finished my CARE sessions with Donna Maples's division, and I think we made some real progress."

"I talked to Donna last evening," Chelsea said, "and she is delighted with what was accomplished through CARE. She was also very impressed with you and the leadership you provided throughout the process."

"Thanks for sharing that with me, Chelsea. It's nice to hear. Donna's a strong manager who needed a refresher in a few areas, which CARE easily addressed. She was a pleasure to work with."

"She told me you spent a lot of time reinforcing the need for adequate and appropriate training."

"That was definitely the main thrust for her division. I think the message got through."

"It certainly did," Matt interjected. "Take a look at this." He handed a single-page document to Charlie.

Donna Maples's Personal CARE Training Program

1. Leadership skills — third quarter
2. ICE: Internal Consulting Expertise — third quarter
3. Marketing via the Internet — fourth quarter
   Budget allocation: $18,000

   Approved by:

"I like the 'approved by' part at the bottom," said Chelsea.

"So do I," Charlie replied. "It means that the boss is completely aware of what training an individual will be taking and has bought into the training program, which will help ensure that the training planned is appropriate."

"By month-end Donna will have approved personal CARE training documents in place for every member of her division," Matt added.

"I'm pleased," Charlie said. "It looks like I can now focus exclusively on Paul Washington's Southern Division."

"Any first impressions?" Matt asked.

"I spent a couple of days with members of Paul's division, and clearly there are a lot of good things happening there. We need to pay some attention to recognition and reward, however. They've got some huge gaps that I'm confident CARE can address."

ZIMCO SOUTHERN DIVISION, DALLAS

When Zack Daniels arrived at Zimco's Southern Division offices that morning, it was with a great deal of anticipation. Zack had been very impressed with the CARE concept that Charlie had presented to the division earlier in the week, so he was thrilled to be part of the team that would be participating in the CARE role-play sessions. He was also pleased that his boss, Paul Washington, was going to participate in the sessions.

Zack turned his attention to the front of the room, where Charlie was finishing his role-play instructions.

"So, in summary, please pay attention to the interaction, as I'll be looking for you to give some constructive criticism to the participants. Now, let's see . . ." Charlie scanned the room. "How about starting with Paul and Zack? Are you guys okay with this?"

"Absolutely," Zack replied.

"Sure," Paul agreed.

Role Play #6
Paul in the role of "Morty"

You are a member of the team that has just pulled together your company's new three-year strategic plan. Your role was to complete the industry analysis section of the document. During the process, Mark, vice-president of corporate strategy, repeatedly emphasized that your analysis would be the foundation on which the corporate strategy would be built. As such, your work was very closely scrutinized by Mark and the rest of the team. To your delight, the corporate strategic plan has been published with your industry analysis summary included, word for word. Because you are also adept at building compelling presentations, Mark had you develop the plan overview presentation, complete with back-up notes. You know from your peers' feedback that you have done an excellent job.

This morning you are to be in the audience while Mark presents the strategic plan to the company's senior executives. Mark is an excellent presenter and you are looking forward to hearing communicated the results of your work and that of your teammates. You are about to enter the conference room when Mark calls you over and tells you there is no need for you to attend the meeting. You and the other members of the team, who wrote the plan, are asked to leave the room before the session starts. You are disappointed, but you do as you are told.

Later on that day, a friend of yours — a vice-president from another division — confirms that Mark did a great job in presenting the strategic plan. You also discover that Mark did not acknowledge any of the people who contributed to development of the plan. Your friend's perception was that Mark had played the key role in bringing the plan to fruition. In fact, he informs you, Mark has been invited to review the industry analysis component of the plan in more detail at the CEO's next meeting. You say nothing to your friend, but inside you are fuming.

Just before the end of the day, you get a call from Mark's assistant, who asks you to meet with Mark before you leave . . .

Zack in the role of "Mark"

You are the vice-president of corporate strategy, and you have been assigned the task of developing the company's new three-year strategic plan. You assembled an excellent team and, under your direction, they developed an outstanding plan, which was extremely well received by the board. In particular, the industry analysis component garnered huge interest and the company's CEO has asked you to review that component in depth at his upcoming meeting. His view is that gaining a better understanding of where your highly competitive, rapidly changing industry is heading will help his senior team in performing their jobs.

This is a big opportunity for you. Your immediate boss, the company's chief operating officer, has told you that the CEO has his eye on you, and that this exposure to the senior brass could be a big stepping stone for your career. You are very conversant with the industry overview, which you presented, but you aren't in a position to provide the kind of in-depth industry review that the CEO has requested. However, you know who can bring you up to speed on what you need to know. You tell your assistant that you need to see Morty as soon as possible . . .

This particular role play was one of Charlie's favorites. He had used it on numerous occasions with terrific success. The role of Mark was tailor-made for Paul Washington. This would be interesting to watch.

"Ready, guys?"

They both nodded in reply.

"Then go to it."

"Morty, come in, please." Mark rises from his desk and gestures toward the couch in the corner. "Have a seat."

Morty does as instructed. "So, things went well today . . . ?"

"At the senior managers' meeting? Yeah, everything went really well. The presentation was very well received. You did a great job building it — thanks."

"You're welcome."

"That's actually why I want to see you. I was asked to

provide a little more information on the industry analysis piece. I was wondering if you could help me out."

There were a couple of moans from the audience. Zack laughed, then looked at Charlie. "Has anybody ever been killed during a role play?"

Charlie chuckled. "Only once. And I removed that one from the book."

After a few more jocular remarks, Charlie quieted the room. "Okay, gang, let's get back to work. Paul, why don't you ask that last question again?"

"Sure."

"Morty, can you help me out with this?"

"What did you have in mind?"

"I was hoping that you could build a presentation for me that would showcase the results of your analysis of our industry."

"Mark, you have my full report. You should be able to pull what you need right from it."

"I could, but I don't have the in-depth knowledge that you've acquired and, quite frankly, I don't have the ability to capture it graphically for a presentation the way you do. You have a talent for using pictures to illustrate what others might use a thousand words for."

"Well . . . I guess I can help. When do you need it by?"

"Could you have it to me by the end of the week?"

Before Morty could reply, Charlie interrupted, "Okay,

guys, what's happening here?"

Alanna Roy replied, "Mark is using Morty, big time."

Charlie turned to Paul. "Paul, do you agree?"

"Well . . . No, I don't think he's using me. I mean, in the role of Morty, I'm really good at what I do, and Mark is taking advantage of my skills. To me, this is just good management. Mark is achieving through others."

"What's missing here? Anybody?"

Zack replied, "Empathy. Mark doesn't give a damn about Morty. He's focused entirely on his own career, and he doesn't realize that the people around him have careers, too."

Alanna chipped in, "Mark needs to understand that it's possible to achieve through others and ensure they get the recognition they deserve at the same time."

"In fact," Zack added, "managers who surround themselves with good people, and then make a point of showcasing their teams' talents and work, make more effective leaders. This has been proven in more than one study."

Charlie looked at Paul Washington. "Put Morty aside for a minute, Paul. How do you feel about what Zack and Alanna just said?"

"I . . . Well, I guess it wasn't too hard for me to understand the role of Mark. This discussion has made me realize that I've maybe been a little too self-serving in the past. I do praise good work, but I . . . I guess I haven't done a good job getting my people's talents exposed to those above me in the organization."

"I think that's an accurate observation. So how

about if you switch over to the role of Mark and see if you can find a better, more empathetic approach to this situation?"

"Sure."

"Morty, I wonder if you can help me?"

"Well . . . maybe. What's up?"

"First, let me tell you that the presentation you built profiling our corporate strategic plan was extremely well received. You have a tremendous knack for using graphics and imagery to bring dry material to life. The senior executive team was very impressed and has fully bought into the strategic direction we've proposed for the corporation."

"Congratulations, Mark. Sounds like you did a wonderful job presenting it."

"I had a lot of confidence in the plan that the team built, so it was pretty easy to deliver the message with passion. The feedback was very positive. Thanks."

"That's great."

"The industry analysis piece that you primed was particularly well received."

"Really?"

"Yeah, so much so that our CEO has asked me to come to his board meeting early next week to deliver an in-depth presentation of this piece alone."

"No kidding . . ."

"What's happening here folks?" Charlie asked.

Ahmed, one of the newest employees in Southern

Division, replied, "Morty can see where this is heading. Mark had memorized the detailed speaking notes that Morty provided with the industry overview slides, and clearly he did a good job representing the quality of the work. But Mark has not read Morty's lengthy, detailed industry review document, and he doesn't have a real understanding of the dynamics that are shaping their industry."

"Good. Okay, then, let's continue," Charlie said to the players.

"Pretty impressive, huh?" Mark says. "So I was —"

"Let me guess. You'd like me to build a presentation, complete with speaking notes, that will bring the detailed analysis to life."

"That's right, but I'd also like you to come with me to the board meeting and deliver the presentation. Would you be comfortable doing that?"

"Well . . . of course. I certainly don't have your presentation skills, but I think I would be okay doing this."

"Morty, I'm confident that you will do an excellent job. You know this material so well, and that's one of the keys to giving a good presentation. Once you've built it, we could do a couple of dry runs, if you like, and I'd be happy to give you a few presentation tips, if you think that would help."

"Mark, that would be really helpful. You're such a good presenter and I know I could learn a lot with your coaching."

"So let's do it. You build it and I'll coach you. Then we'll go to the board meeting together and blow them away."

"Deal."

"Oh, Morty — one more thing. The boss tells me I'm in line for a promotion soon. If and when that happens, I'll be recommending that he put you into my job. You've got a great mind and you'd be perfect in the role of vice-president, corporate strategy."

"Oh, Mark." Morty runs to him and gives him a big hug.

The role-play observers burst out laughing, none louder than Charlie. "Okay," Charlie said, "I think that's a wrap."

The audience applauded the role-players' efforts and Paul and Zack sat down.

"Any comments or observations?" Charlie asked.

"Certainly," Zack said. "I have to admit that it sure felt good to have my boss put some effort into show-casing my abilities, and helping me achieve my goals. I'd say my loyalty-to-boss level went up dramatically."

"Paul, how about you?"

"Charlie, I really learned a lot today. I've often seen managers bring their direct reports to a meeting to present projects for which the managers are ultimately responsible. I used to think this was a sign of weakness — that they didn't have the ability or the confidence to present the material themselves."

"How do you feel now?"

"More likely I was seeing empathetic managers, who were confident enough in their own skills to showcase those of the people with whom they work."

"You've hit on a very interesting point, which I can illustrate with a little story," said Charlie. "Eons ago, when I was a young manager, I worked with a fellow named Mickey, who was much like Mark in the first part of our role play. Mickey was a very bright guy, and I thought he would shoot through the management ranks right to the top. He was one of those people who get referred to as 'the guy we'll all be working for some day.' Mickey never achieved his potential, however, and he finished his career in lower middle management.

"It wasn't until years later, when I developed and started to apply the CARE concept, that I understood what had kept Mickey from realizing his potential. He came across as a one-man show. And as a one-man show, in the eyes of his many bosses over the years he rendered himself indispensable. It was as if everyone thought, 'We can't afford to move or promote Mickey, because he's too important where he is and he'll be almost impossible to replace.'"

"So by always taking center stage and not exposing his people to those above him, he killed his own career," Paul said.

"Exactly. In the eyes of the people above him, there was never a logical candidate to replace Mickey."

"He didn't have a succession plan," Zack concluded.

"That's a good way of putting it, Zack," Charlie replied. "Empathy ensures that you are always looking for opportunities to help the people around you achieve their goals, which may very well include career advancement. An empathetic manager ensures that the people on his or her team receive public recognition for the quality work they do. Empathetic managers groom and showcase natural successors, which then releases the managers for opportunities that afford them career advancement."

"CARE can really help the boss and the employee reach their career goals," Paul concluded.

"Everyone wins," Charlie agreed.

12

Reward

During the lunch break, Charlie observed an energy and warmth among the participants that certainly hadn't been there when the CARE training started in Paul Washington's division. Paul in particular was like a new man.

Charlie had seen this kind of reaction to CARE training many times before. It was tremendously rewarding to know that the concept he had developed so many years ago could still make a difference. In a world that moved so very fast, it was comforting to know that some things stayed the same.

The old man looked at his watch. One more session to go and, save for his final report to Matt McMaster, his work at Zimco would be done. He had really enjoyed the last several weeks, but he was also getting a little tired.

Charlie tapped on the table to get the team's attention. It was time to reconvene. The members of Paul's division still had a few things to learn about the importance of rewards.

"Any volunteers for this next role play?"

Everyone's hand went up. Charlie smiled. "Lots of hams in this group." He looked at his list. "Millie, you haven't had a chance yet. And Rollie, how about you?" Millie and Rollie both nodded in agreement.

Role Play #7
Millie in the role of "Bertha"

You are vice-president of the sales organization in your company. You are coming off a bad year, and you have just finished a rough first quarter. Your boss, the company's president, is putting pressure on you to improve your results — or else. Friends have told you that the rumor mill is buzzing with news that your boss has recently met with a headhunter. The word is that he is looking for somebody to replace you.

You're confident you can turn the ship around, based on the sales opportunities in your pending funnel, but history tells you that you can't afford to get overly optimistic. Last quarter looked equally promising, but four large deals that you expected to close fell through. The most frustrating thing is that the deals weren't lost because of the sales propositions presented to your clients. They fell through for two reasons: you weren't able to get bid responses to the clients on time, which automatically rendered you non-compliant with the bid terms and eliminated a sales opportunity, and you could not commit to delivery of the solutions required consistent with the customers' demands. It's become clear to you that your salespeople are doing their jobs, but the pre- and post-sales technical team, which also reports to you, is not doing theirs.

The general manager responsible for technical support, Murdock, is a good guy, but you can't survive in your job unless his department cleans up its act and starts doing its job. The salespeople are upset because they are losing deals and commissions, and last week two of your best sales representatives resigned. Morale is low, and relations between the sales and technical support organizations are poor at best. You decide to have it out with Murdock. He either gets his department to deliver or he gets replaced . . .

Rollie in the role of "Murdock"

You are the general manager responsible for pre- and post-sales technical support. The function you provide is absolutely critical to the sales success of your company, because the products and services you sell are highly technical.

During the last few years, the technology architecture on which your products are based has changed dramatically. The world has become increasingly digital and networked, and everything you touch today demands that your people be conversant with Internet protocol, or IP, as it's commonly known.

You are funded for a total of 90 technical resource people, most of whom are engineers and computer science graduates. For the last year and a half, however, you have never had more than 75 people on staff at any one time. The skills your people have are in tremendous demand, and you are constantly being raided by technical recruiting organizations that want to hire your people. The headhunters have done their jobs extremely well. Tempted by excellent salaries and terrific bonus and stock-option plans, your people are leaving in droves. You are hiring as fast as you can, but you are clearly fighting a losing battle. Last month you hired 11 new engineers, all right out of school — and you received 14 resignations.

The problem, you know, has nothing to do with you or your company. It has to do with the current compensation plan. The base pay levels for your IP-knowledgeable resource people are well below market value and, per-haps more important, their bonus plan is a joke. The members of your team are every bit as important as the sales team in the sales process, yet they are not eligible for any commission or bonus based on sales. As the last engineer who resigned said, "I have difficulty watching the rep I support bring in more in commissions than I made in salary, when I was the guy who closed most of his deals." While you acknowledge that the salespeople play a more important role than the engineer gave them credit for, you do believe there is a grain of truth in what he said. Your people are underpaid in today's market.

You receive a call to meet with your boss, Bertha, the vice-president of sales. You're certain that she wants to lean on you because of the level of support your team is providing. It's a conversation you have had before with every one of the sales managers, so you're not surprised that Bertha has now jumped on this issue. Your answers to her questions will be the same that you gave to your peers: "I can't do the work when we don't have the people."

You arrive at Bertha's office at the agreed-upon time. She is reviewing her results reports and she appears to be in a foul mood . . .

"Hmm, Bertha sounds like a monster. I'm thinking maybe I don't want to do this role-play after all," Rollie said.

Millie laughed the loudest. "Get your incompetent butt in here now — and don't give me any lip!"

"Okay, has everybody finished reading the role-play scenarios?" There were nods around the room, so Charlie continued. "This one is always fun. Murdock, Bertha — let's do it."

Bertha puts down the reports she is perusing. "Come in, Murdock. Have a seat."

Murdock sits down opposite Bertha's desk. "You wanted to see me?"

"Yes. Have you seen last quarter's results?"

"Unfortunately, yes. Another dismal quarter."

"I'm afraid so." Bertha takes a deep breath and lets it out slowly. "Look, I'm not going to beat around the bush, Murdock. Your team is not doing the job we need to succeed in this marketplace. We are missing bid opportunities left, right, and center, and the ones we are bidding on — well, half of those we're losing out on because we can't meet the customers' delivery time frames. I am really, really frustrated over this. Quite frankly, my job is more than likely in jeopardy because of our poor results. And believe me, if I lose my job, I'll be taking a few people out before I go!"

"Okay, let's pause here for a moment," Charlie said. He addressed the role-play observers, "Any thoughts or comments here?"

Marcia Raddington, a novice manager, replied, "I'm pretty new as a manager, but it seems to me that Bertha is coming down hard on Murdock without giving him a chance to explain why his department is having difficulty delivering on its commitments."

"She's not . . . ?"

"Living in his shoes, or empathizing."

"Excellent," Charlie replied. "Murdock, how are you feeling right now?"

"I'm pretty angry. I don't think Big Bertha here is really being fair to me, and I particularly do not appreciate the parental scolding I'm getting. I'm thinking really hard about telling Bertha to take this job and —"

"Okay, I think we get the picture," Charlie chuckled. "Bertha, how about you?"

"I guess I can relate to what Murdock is saying, but quite frankly I have a reason to be angry. His team is not performing and I'm in jeopardy of losing my job as a result."

"Do you know why his team is not performing?" Charlie asked.

"No . . . I guess maybe I should —"

"Put yourself in his shoes —"

"— and find out."

"Exactly."

"Let's do a re-start on this one . . ."

Bertha steps out from behind her desk when Murdock enters her office. "Hi, Murdock. How are things?"

"I think we both know they've been better."

"Yeah, we're on the same page on this one." Bertha points to the captain's chairs in the corner of her office. "Have a seat."

"Thanks." Murdock sits down and his boss joins him.

"So we both know we're in a pretty tough spot right now, and we need some solutions."

"You're right. Our last quarter's results were very poor, and even though we have some good opportunities this quarter, I'm afraid we're going to lose out because of our inability to deliver. I —"

"Murdock," Bertha interrupts, "explain this to me, please. How can we be falling down on the job like this? Your team's performance is killing us!"

"Bertha, it's not my team's performance that is the root of the problem."

Bertha's exasperation is evident in her tone. "Then what is it?"

"It's our industry. We haven't kept pace with the changes in our industry."

"I don't think I understand . . ."

"Bertha, we've worked together for five years, and in the first four years we delivered outstanding results."

"You're right, but those past successes aren't all that relevant, given our recent track record."

"I know that, but what I also know is that our industry has been totally transformed in the last 24 months, and we haven't kept pace."

"In what way?"

"Three years ago, the technology team's role in the sales process was relatively minor. Today, thanks to the emergence of networked products and the Internet, the role my team plays is absolutely critical to our success."

"And . . . ?"

"And we don't reward our people based on their contribution."

"I don't understand."

"Look, my resource base is constantly turning over because my people are getting much more lucrative offers from the street. Last year, my retention rate was a lousy 62 percent. I can't hire people fast enough to replace the ones I'm losing. And with the salary scale I have to work with, I can only attract recent graduates. Now, a year after hiring them, I'm starting to lose some of these people. We've become a training ground for our competitors."

"Why haven't you talked to me about this?"

"Bertha, I've raised it on several occasions and, quite frankly, it's fallen on deaf ears."

Bertha pauses. "I . . . I do recall you talking about raising the base pay of our technical staff to market value, then putting them on the sales commission plan, or a similar plan of some sort."

"And, not to be critical, my proposal was never given

any real consideration."

"Murdock, I don't think that's a totally fair statement. It was considered, but, if I recall correctly, it was going to raise our operating expenses by close to two million dollars a year."

"That's right, but it would have given us the technical capacity we need to meet and beat our sales forecasts. And, Bertha, do you know how much we spent last year recruiting and training new engineers?"

"No, how much?"

"Two million dollars."

"Let's stop right here, guys," Charlie said. "That was excellent. Millie, what have you learned?"

"That it's important to ensure people are rewarded for what they contribute to the success of the team."

"And if people are properly rewarded for what they do, they will deliver better overall performance," Paul Washington added.

"Let me tell you a little more about this particular situation," Charlie said. "This role play, like many of them, as I mentioned earlier, is based on a real situation. It's been updated to make it relevant to today's world, of course, but it's a situation in which I was involved as a very young factory worker, before I developed CARE. Without going into all the details, the factory support people were ultimately placed on the sales compensation plan, and the results were outstanding."

"Things turned around?" Millie asked.

"The vacant factory positions were filled within

weeks of modifying our pay structure, and employee attrition disappeared virtually overnight. We not only met our second-quarter numbers, we delivered record sales revenues for the year. The experience helped me understand the importance of properly rewarding people for their efforts. I suppose it's why I included reward as an integral part of CARE."

"I've certainly learned a lot from this experience," Rollie said. "Thanks."

"You're welcome. Paul, how do you feel now about the reward programs available to members of your division?"

"Charlie, I am very excited by this and, frankly, by everything that I've learned this past week. I'd say that our entire reward program needs to be revisited. I suspect that there are a few areas that could use a little CARE."

"There always are, Paul," the older man replied. "There always are."

13

In Praise of Grandpa Charlie

Matt McMaster was looking forward to Zimco's board meeting. Matt had been company president for just over a year now, and this was the first quarter in which he was able to show concrete evidence of the progress the company had made in the past year. Revenues were up and operating costs were down. The company was cash-positive in the last quarter and had even eaten into its long-term debt.

More important, the financial impact of the major new contracts that Zimco had just been awarded were not even reflected yet in the company's financials. The stock market had taken note of Zimco's first steps toward a successful turnaround. The company's stock had risen 27 percent in the last three months, and several major analysts rated it a strong buy. Matt knew that his job of saving Zimco was not yet done, but the trend was clearly positive. Matt also recognized the foundation on which Zimco's new-found success had been built — CARE.

Matt reviewed for the last time the presentation that he would soon deliver to Zimco's board of directors. He stopped when he got to the slide that illustrated the results of the annual employee survey.

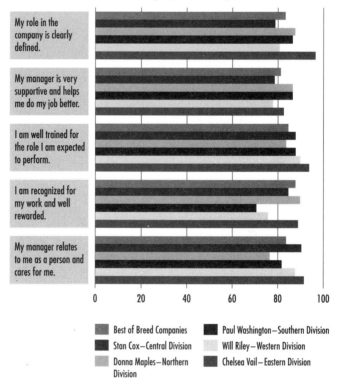

This was the slide that best demonstrated the power of CARE. He recalled the poor results of the survey done shortly after his arrival. Now every division was creating and delivering employee value at a level comparable to that of Chelsea Vail's division. This, Matt knew, was the primary reason for the turnaround. A lot of other changes had certainly been made, but more than anything else it was CARE, and the resulting tremendous increase in employee value, that had caused the turnaround in Zimco's fortunes.

Matt had signed a three-year contract, but in today's world that didn't constitute job security. He knew that presidents and CEOs are dispensed with as easily as coaches are fired in the world of sports. However, the board presentation went extremely well, as Matt had expected, and the directors gave him a strong mandate to continue in his current capacity.

Matt slipped into his car and pulled out of the parking lot. He was looking forward to a well-deserved round of golf with a new friend — and a forever mentor — Grandpa Charlie.

Charlie knew that his game had slipped a little in the last year, but today he felt pretty good. His back had held up well during his warm-up, and the weather was hot, the way he preferred it. He had played Matt McMaster on only one other occasion, the day they met. It seemed much longer than a year and a bit ago.

On the practice green Charlie rolled in a fifteen-foot putt.

"I guess you'll be giving me strokes today."

Charlie looked up to see the smiling face of Matt McMaster. "In your dreams, kid. In your dreams."

The two men arrived at the eighteenth green in a dead heat. Charlie was having his best game in years, but

Matt was equal to the task.

The older man watched as his opponent's birdie-putt rolled past the final hole. Matt tapped it in for his par. Charlie needed to hole his eighteen-foot birdie-putt to win, and he needed to two-putt for a tie.

He lined up the fast downhill putt and tapped it gently. It rolled slowly at first, picked up speed, and then found the heart of the hole. "Yes!" Charlie pumped his fist in the manner of today's golfing youth.

His hand extended, Matt approached his mentor and congratulated him. "I can't believe you made that putt. Congratulations, Charlie. Today, you are the better man."

Charlie winked at Matt McMaster. "What do you mean, today?"

Matt laughed and slipped his arm around Charlie's shoulders. "C'mon, let me buy you a beer."

The greeting Charlie received when he entered the clubhouse was overwhelming. Well over a hundred employees of Zimco were in the lounge, and they rose in unison to cheer him. The banner on the back wall of the room said what all of them were thinking:

Thanks for teaching us how to CARE!
You're the best, Grandpa Charlie!

One by one, the people of Zimco came up to Charlie to thank him for the contribution he had made to their firm and to their lives. He was overcome. Finally the person he most wanted to see appeared in front of him. He embraced his granddaughter warmly. "You're behind this, I'm sure."

She returned the hug and said, "I had nothing to do with it, I swear. But you deserve every bit of recognition you are getting today. You and CARE have made such a difference." As she broke from his embrace, she added, "I am so incredibly proud of you, Grandpa. I love you."

Charlie's eyes misted over. "I love you too, Chelsea. I love you too."

14

Three Years of CARE

It was unusual for the chairman of the board to contact Matt between board meetings, especially about operational issues. So Matt was surprised when his calendar showed a meeting with Robin Meadows. He slipped out of his office to check with his assistant.

"Auburn, do you have any idea what this meeting with Robin is about?"

"I asked his assistant, but she said she didn't know, just that he wanted to see you sometime today."

Matt was puzzled. "Okay, thanks. I guess I'll find out when he gets here."

He returned to his office and reflected on what Robin could possibly want. Matt had recently presented his new three-year plan to the board, and it had been extremely well received. No wonder — Zimco was experiencing record growth, the company had retired its long-term debt, and its stock was among the top ten performers on the New York Stock Exchange. He had led Zimco to a very impressive turnaround in his three-plus years as its president, and had made a lot of people a lot of money along the way. Things simply could not be better.

❖

Chelsea Vail was anxious for her day to be over. She had a very important date that evening, one that she was really looking forward to. Grandpa Charlie was turning 82 and, in his own words, was still going strong. She was taking him out to one of his favorite restaurants. It would be an enjoyable evening.

Chelsea was packing her things up, getting ready to leave, when the phone rang. She thought of letting the voice-mail system take over, but at the last minute she picked up the receiver.

"Chelsea Vail speaking . . . Well, I was just heading out . . . Oh . . . Okay, I guess that would be okay. . . . No, I already have dinner plans with my Grandpa Charlie . . . Sure. I can call him and let him know I'll be a tad late. . . . Okay, I'll see you in twenty."

Chelsea hung up the phone. Now what could this be all about?

Charlie checked his watch. Chelsea had called to say she would be roughly half an hour late, but it had now been almost an hour. He hoped that everything was all right. He signaled to the waiter, planning to check whether his granddaughter had perhaps called, but just then she walked into the restaurant. She looked radiant.

He stood to greet her. "I thought you were going to stand me up," he said as he hugged her warmly.

"Not a chance. Besides, what kind of company president would I be if I stood up the very guy who helped me get there?"

"What . . . ?"

Her eyes were sparkling with excitement. "Yes, Grandpa, yes! Matt has been asked to take on a bigger company in our corporate family. I've been appointed as the new president of Zimco."

"My God, girl, you did it!" he exclaimed. "You did it!"

"We did it, Grandpa, the three of us!"

"The three of us?"

"The three of us — you, me, and CARE!"